Mike McGrath

Python

2nd edition

In easy steps is an imprint of In Easy Steps Limited
16 Hamilton Terrace · Holly Walk · Leamington Spa
Warwickshire · United Kingdom · CV32 4LY
www.ineasysteps.com

Second Edition

Notice of Liability
Every effort has been made to ensure that this book contains accurate
and current information. However, In Easy Steps Limited and the
author shall not be liable for any loss or damage suffered by readers
as a result of any information contained herein.

Trademarks
All trademarks are acknowledged as belonging to their respective
companies.

In Easy Steps Limited supports The Forest Stewardship Council (FSC),
the leading international forest certification organization. All our titles
that are printed on Greenpeace approved FSC certified paper carry the
FSC logo.

MIX
Paper from
responsible sources
FSC® C020837

Printed and bound in the United Kingdom

ISBN 978-1-84078-812-9

Contents

Preface

The creation of this book has been for me, Mike McGrath, an exciting personal journey in discovering how Python can be used today for procedural and object-oriented programming, to develop applications and to provide online functionality. Example code listed in this book describes how to produce Python programs **in easy steps** – and the screenshots illustrate the actual results. I sincerely hope you enjoy discovering the exciting possibilities of Python, and have as much fun with it as I did in writing this book.

In order to clarify the code listed in the steps given in each example I have adopted certain colorization conventions. Components of the Python programming language are colored blue, programmer-specified names are red, numeric and string data values are black, and comments are green, like this:

```
# Write the traditional greeting.
greeting = 'Hello World!'
print( greeting )
```

Additionally, in order to identify each source code file described in the steps, a colored icon and file name appears in the margin alongside the steps:

script.py   page.html   image.gif

For convenience I have placed source code files from the examples featured in this book into a single ZIP archive. You can obtain the complete archive by following these easy steps:

1. Browse to **www.ineasysteps.com** then navigate to Free Resources and choose the Downloads section

2. Find Python in easy steps, 2nd edition in the list, then click on the hyperlink entitled All Code Examples to download the archive

3. Next, extract the **MyScripts** and **MyProjects** folders to your home directory (such as **C:**) and copy all contents of the **htdocs** folder to your web server's documents directory

4. Now, follow the steps to call upon the Python interpreter and see the output

You will also find updates, if any, to this book in the Downloads section for this book.

1 Getting started

Welcome to the exciting world of the Python programming language. This chapter demonstrates how to install Python and create your first program.

Discover all the latest
Python news online at
www.python.org

Programming languages
that group blocks by
indentation are said to
adhere to the "offside
rule" – a pun on the
offside rule in soccer.

Introducing Python

Python is a high-level (human-readable) programming language
that is processed by the Python "interpreter" to produce results.
Python includes a comprehensive standard library of tested code
modules that can be easily incorporated into your own programs.

The Python language was developed by Guido van Rossum in the
late eighties and early nineties at the National Research Institute
for Mathematics and Computer Science in the Netherlands.
Python is derived from many other languages, including C,
C++, the Unix shell and other programming languages. Today,
Python is maintained by a core development team at the Institute,
although Guido van Rossum still holds a vital role in directing its
progress.

The basic philosophy of the Python language is readability, which
makes it particularly well-suited for beginners in computer
programming, and it can be summarized by these principles:

- Beautiful is better than ugly.

- Explicit is better than implicit.

- Simple is better than complex.

- Complex is better than complicated.

- Readability counts.

As Python is intended to be highly readable, it uses English
keywords frequently where other languages may use punctuation.
Most significantly, it uses indentation to group together
statements into code "blocks", whereas other languages may use
keywords or punctuation for this purpose. For example, in the
Pascal programming language, blocks start with the keyword
begin and end with the keyword **end**, and in the C programming
language, blocks are enclosed within curly brackets (**{ }** braces).
Grouping blocks of statements by indentation is sometimes
criticized by programmers familiar with languages that group
by punctuation, but the use of indentation in Python certainly
produces code that has an uncluttered visual layout.

Some of Python's key distinguishing features that make it an attractive choice of language for the beginner include:

- **Python is free** – is open source distributable software.

- **Python is easy to learn** – has a simple language syntax.

- **Python is easy to read** – is uncluttered by punctuation.

- **Python is easy to maintain** – is modular for simplicity.

- **Python is "batteries included"** – provides a large standard library for easy integration into your own programs.

- **Python is interactive** – has a terminal for debugging and testing snippets of code.

- **Python is portable** – runs on a wide variety of hardware platforms and has the same interface on all platforms.

- **Python is interpreted** – there is no compilation required.

- **Python is high-level** – has automatic memory management.

- **Python is extensible** – allows the addition of low-level modules to the interpreter for customization.

- **Python is versatile** – supports both procedure-orientated programming and object-orientated programming (OOP).

- **Python is flexible** – can create console programs, windowed GUI (Graphical User Interface) applications, and CGI (Common Gateway Interface) scripts to process web data.

Python is named after the British television comedy series "Monty Python's Flying Circus" – you may encounter references to this in the Python documentation.

As development of Python continues, newer versions are released as with most software. Currently, the final 2.7 version is out, with a statement of extended support for this end-of-life release. The 2.x branch will see no new major releases after that.

The 3.x branch is under active development and has already seen several stable releases. This means that all recent standard library improvements, for example, are only available in Python 3.x. This book describes and demonstrates features of the present and the future of Python with the latest 3.x version.

Python 3.x is not backward compatible with Python 2.7.

Installing Python on Windows

Before you can begin programming in the Python language you need to install the Python interpreter on your computer, and the standard library of tested code modules that comes along with it. This is available online as a free download from the Python website at **https://python.org/downloads**. For Windows users there are installers available in both 32-bit and 64-bit versions:

 Launch a web browser, then navigate to **python.org/downloads** and download the appropriate installer for your system – in this example it's a file named "python-3.7.0.exe"

 When the download completes, run the installer and check the "Add Python 3.7 to PATH" option

Installers for macOS/Mac OS X in 32-bit and 64-bit versions are available at **python.org/downloads**

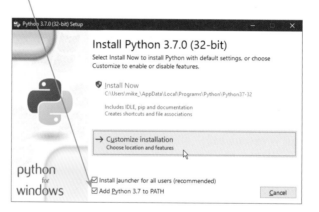

Next, click the "Customize installation" option

Check all "Optional Features" options, then click **Next**

Be sure to check the option to install "pip" so you can easily install Python packages later.

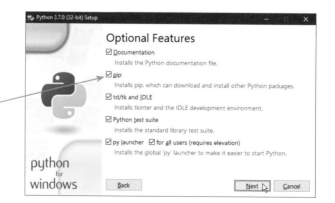

5 Now, change the lengthy suggested installation location to a more simple location of "C:\Python37"

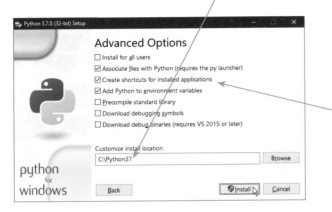

Accept the suggested features in the Advanced Options dialog – as illustrated here.

6 Click on **Install** to begin copying files onto your PC, then click the **Close** button to complete the installation

7 To confirm Python is now available, launch a Command Prompt window (run **cmd.exe**) and precisely enter the command **python -V** – the Python interpreter should respond with its version number

The letter V in the command <u>must</u> be uppercase. Ensure the command responds with the version number before proceeding to the examples in this book.

Installing Python on Linux

Linux distributions will, typically, include Python but generally have the 2.7 version as their default. For development on the 3.x branch of Python releases you will probably have to install the latest release alongside the default version.

 1 Launch a terminal window and precisely enter this command to reveal the installed default Python version
python -V

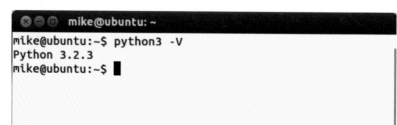

```
mike@ubuntu: ~
mike@ubuntu:~$ python -V
Python 2.7.3
mike@ubuntu:~$
```

 2 Next, precisely enter this command to reveal the default version of a Python 3.x branch, if any is installed
python3 -V

```
mike@ubuntu: ~
mike@ubuntu:~$ python3 -V
Python 3.2.3
mike@ubuntu:~$
```

3 Now, launch your Linux system's package manager to see if a later Python version is available for installation – for example use the Software Center on Ubuntu systems

Ubuntu Software Center

Consult your Linux distro's documentation for further help on installing Python.

Beware

Don't remove the default 2.7 version of Python from your system in case some applications depend upon it.

12

4 Search for "python" in the package manager to see what Python versions and components are installed, or if later versions are available for installation

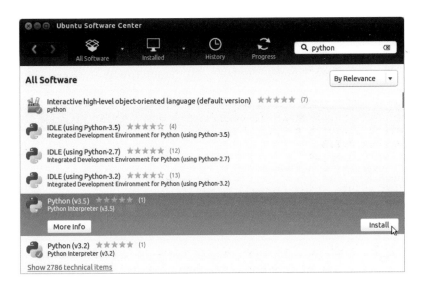

You may also, optionally, install IDLE for Python 3.5, but this is not an absolute requirement as the Python programming examples in this book are all created in a plain text editor such as Nano.

5 Finally, install the latest version of the Python 3.x branch for Linux – in this case it's Python 3.5

6 To confirm the latest version of Python is now available on your computer launch a Terminal window and precisely enter this explicit command
python3 -V

```
mike@ubuntu: ~
mike@ubuntu:~$ python3 -V
Python 3.5.2
mike@ubuntu:~$
```

You can now use the command **python3** to have that version of the Python interpreter process your programs.

13

Meeting the interpreter

The Python interpreter processes text-based program code, and also has an interactive mode where you can test snippets of code and is useful for debugging code. Python's interactive mode can be entered in a number of ways:

- From a regular Command Prompt – simply enter the command **python** to produce the Python primary prompt **>>>** where you can interact with the interpreter.

Command Prompt

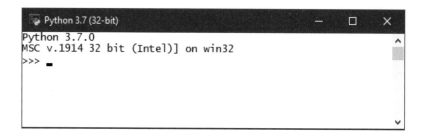

```
Command Prompt - python                    —    □    ✕
Microsoft Windows [Version 10.0.17134.81]
(c) 2018 Microsoft Corporation. All rights reserved.

C:\Users\mike_>python
Python 3.7.0
[MSC v.1914 32 bit (Intel)] on win32
>>> ▂
```

- From the Start Menu – choose "Python" (command line) to open a window containing the Python **>>>** primary prompt.

Python
(command line)

```
Python 3.7 (32-bit)                        —    □    ✕
Python 3.7.0
MSC v.1914 32 bit (Intel)] on win32
>>> ▂
```

- From the Start Menu – choose "IDLE" (Python GUI) to launch a Python Shell window containing the Python **>>>** primary prompt.

IDLE
(Python GUI)

```
Python 3.7.0 Shell                         —    □    ✕
File  Edit  Shell  Debug  Options  Window  Help
Python 3.7.0
[MSC v.1914 32 bit (Intel)] on win32
Type "copyright", "credits" or "license()" for more
information.
>>> |
                                              Ln: 3  Col: 4
```

Irrespective of the method used to enter interactive mode, the Python interpreter will respond in the same way to commands entered at its **>>>** primary prompt. In its simplest form, the interpreter can be used as a calculator.

 Enter Python interactive mode, using any method outlined opposite, then type a simple addition and hit Return to see the interpreter print out the sum total

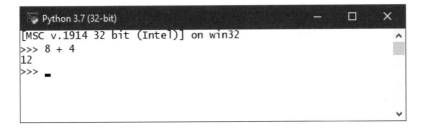

```
Python 3.7 (32-bit)                              —    □    X
[MSC v.1914 32 bit (Intel)] on win32
>>> 8 + 4
12
>>>
```

The Python interpreter also understands expressions, so parentheses can be used to give higher precedence – the part of the expression enclosed within parentheses will be calculated first.

2 Next, at the Python prompt enter an expression with three components without specifying any precedence order

```
Python 3.7 (32-bit)                              —    □    X
>>> 3 * 8 + 4
28
>>>
```

3 Now, at the Python prompt enter the same expression but add parentheses to specify precedence order

```
Python 3.7 (32-bit)                              —    □    X
>>> 3 * ( 8 + 4 )
36
>>>
```

Hot tip

Spaces in expressions are ignored, so 8+4 can be also be entered with added spaces for clarity – as illustrated here.

Don't forget

Interactive mode is mostly used to test snippets of code and for debugging code.

Beware

"IDLE" is an acronym for Python's Integrated DeveLopment Environment, but has limited features so is not used to demonstrate examples in this book.

Writing your first program

Python's interactive mode is useful as a simple calculator, but you can create programs for more extensive functionality. A Python program is simply a plain text file script created with an editor, such as Windows' Notepad, that has been saved with a ".py" file extension. Python programs can be executed by stating the script file name after the **python** command at a terminal prompt.

The traditional first program to create when learning any programming language simply prints out a specified greeting message. In Python, the **print()** function is used to specify the message within its parentheses. This must be a string of characters enclosed between quote marks. These may be " " double quote marks or ' ' single quote marks – but not a mixture of both.

Beware

Don't use a word processor to create program files as they add format information to the file.

hello.py

 On Windows, launch any plain text editor such as the Notepad application

 Next, precisely type the following statement into the empty text editor window
print('Hello World!')

 Now, create a new directory at **C:\MyScripts** and save the file in it as **hello.py**

```
hello.py - Notepad
File  Edit  Format  View  Help
print( 'Hello World!' )
```

Hot tip

The directory created at **C:\MyScripts** will be used to contain all Windows examples in this book.

4 Finally, launch a Command Prompt window, navigate to the new directory and precisely enter the command **python hello.py** – to see the Python interpreter run your program and print out the specified greeting message

```
Command Prompt
C:\MyScripts>python hello.py
Hello World!

C:\MyScripts>_
```

16

The procedure to create the traditional first Python program is identical on Linux systems to that on Windows systems. It is, however, important to be aware, on any platform where different versions of Python are installed: you must use the correct command to call upon the particular Python interpreter required. This is especially important on Linux systems that often ship with the Python 2.7 version installed as their default. This means that the command **python** will assume you want to call that interpreter. Where Python 3.3 is installed, and you want to call that particular interpreter to process a script, you must use the command **python3.3** to explicitly call upon that version's interpreter.

 On Linux, launch any plain text editor such as the Nano application

hello.py

2   Next, precisely type the following statement into the empty text editor window
print('Hello World!')

3   Now, save the file in your home directory as **hello.py**

```
😣➖🔲   mike@ubuntu: ~
 GNU nano              New Buffer              Modified

print( 'Hello World!' )
```

4   Finally, launch a Terminal window and navigate to your home directory and precisely enter the command **python3.3 hello.py** – to see the Python interpreter run your program and print out the specified greeting message

```
😣➖🔲   mike@ubuntu: ~
mike@ubuntu:~$ python3 hello.py
Hello World!
mike@ubuntu:~$
```

All further examples in this book are illustrated on Windows (simply because that platform has the most users) but they can also be created and executed on Linux.

17

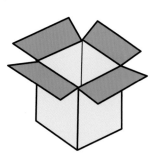

Employing variables

In programming, a "variable" is a container in which a data value can be stored within the computer's memory. The stored value can then be referenced using the variable's name. The programmer can choose any name for a variable, except the Python keywords listed on the inside front cover of this book, and it is good practice to choose meaningful names that reflect the variable's content.

Data to be stored in a variable is assigned in a Python program declaration statement with the = assignment operator. For example, to store the numeric value eight in a variable named "a":

`a = 8`

String data must be enclosed within quote marks to denote the start and end of the string.

The stored value can then be referenced using the variable's name, so that the statement **print(a)** will output the stored value **8**. That variable can subsequently be assigned a different value, so its value can vary as the program proceeds – hence the term "variable".

In Python programming, a variable must be assigned an initial value ("initialized") in the statement that declares it in a program – otherwise the interpreter will report a "not defined" error.

Multiple variables can be initialized with a common value in a single statement using a sequence of = assignments. For example, to initialize variables named "a", "b" and "c", each with a numeric value of eight, like this:

`a = b = c = 8`

Alternatively, multiple variables can be initialized with differing values in a single statement using comma separators. For example, to initialize variables named "a", "b" and "c" with numeric values of one, two and three respectively, like this:

`a , b , c = 1 , 2 , 3`

Hot tip

Programming languages that require variable types to be specified are alternatively known as "strongly typed" whereas those that do not are alternatively known as "loosely typed".

Some programming languages, such as Java, demand you specify what type of data a variable may contain in its declaration. This reserves a specific amount of memory space and is known as "static typing". Python variables, on the other hand, have no such limitation and adjust the memory allocation to suit the various data values assigned to their variables ("dynamic typing"). This means they can store integer whole numbers, floating-point numbers, text strings, or Boolean values of **True** or **False** as required.

Optionally, comments can be added to your Python scripts to describe the purpose of statements or sections of code if preceded by a **#** hash character. Everything following the **#** hash character up to the end of the line is ignored by the Python interpreter. It is useful to comment your code to make its purpose clear to others or when revisiting the code yourself later.

1 Launch a plain text editor, then declare and initialize a variable – then display its stored value
```
# Initialize a variable with an integer value.
var = 8
print( var )
```

var.py

2 Next, assign a new value and display that stored value
```
# Assign a float value to the variable.
var = 3.142
print( var )
```

3 Now, assign a different value and display the stored value
```
# Assign a string value to the variable.
var = 'Python in easy steps'
print( var )
```

4 Finally, assign another value and display the stored value
```
# Assign a boolean value to the variable.
var = True
print( var )
```

5 Save the file in your scripts directory, then open a Command Prompt window there and run the program – to see the stored values output as the program proceeds

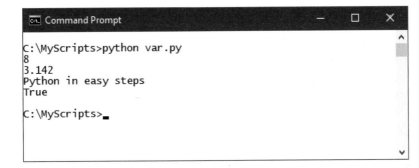

```
C:\MyScripts>python var.py
8
3.142
Python in easy steps
True

C:\MyScripts>
```

19

Hot tip

Multi-line comments can be added to a script if enclosed between triple quote marks """...""" .

Obtaining user input

Just as a data value can be assigned to a variable in a Python script, a user-specified value can be assigned to a variable with the Python **input()** function. This accepts a string within its parentheses that will prompt the user for input by displaying that string then wait to read a line of input.

User input is read as a text string, even when it's numeric, and can be assigned to a variable using the = assignment operator as usual. The value assigned to any variable can be displayed by specifying the variable name to the **print()** function – to reference that variable's stored value.

Multiple values to be displayed can be specified to the **print()** function as a comma-separated list within its parentheses.

1 Launch a plain text editor, then declare and initialize a variable by requesting user input
# Initialize a variable with a user-specified value.
user = input('I am Python. What is your name? : ')

2 Next, display a response message confirming the input by referencing the stored user name
# Output a string and a variable value.
print('Welcome' , user)

3 Now, save the file in your scripts directory then open a Command Prompt window there and run this program – enter your name, then hit Return to see the response message include your name

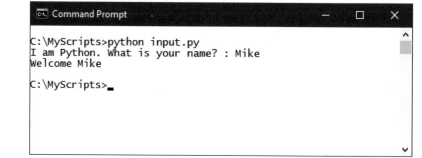

```
C:\MyScripts>python input.py
I am Python. What is your name? : Mike
Welcome Mike

C:\MyScripts>
```

input.py

Hot tip

Notice that the prompt string ends with a space that is displayed in output – so the user entry is separated from the colon when typed in.

When multiple values are specified to the **print()** function it will display each value in output separated by a single space by default. An alternative separator can, however, be specified by adding a **sep** parameter to the comma-separated list. For example, **sep = '*'** will display each value in output separated by an asterisk character.

Output displayed by the **print()** function will, by default, add an invisible \n newline character at the end of the line to automatically move the print head to the next line. An alternative line ending can, however, be specified by adding an **end** parameter to the comma-separated list. For example, **end = '!'** will display each value in output then end the line with an exclamation mark.

You can explicitly specify a newline to the **end** parameter; for example, **end='!\n'** adds both an exclamation mark and a newline character.

4 Edit the script to declare and initialize a second variable by requesting more user input

```
# Initialize another variable with a user-specified value.
lang = input( 'Favorite programming language? : ' )
```

5 Next, display a response message confirming the input by referencing the stored language name – and specifying a custom separator and a custom line ending

```
# Output a string and a variable value.
print( lang , 'Is' , 'Fun' , sep = ' * ' , end = '!\n' )
```

6 Now, save the file once more, then open a Command Prompt window there and run this program again – enter your name and a programming language, then hit Return to see the response message include your user input

```
Command Prompt                           —    □    ×

C:\MyScripts>python input.py
I am Python. What is your name? : Mike
Welcome Mike
Favorite programming language? : Python
Python * Is * Fun!

C:\MyScripts>_
```

You can include space characters around the separator character for clarity – like those shown around the asterisk character in this example.

Correcting errors

In Python programming there are three types of error that can occur. It is useful to recognize the different error types so they can be corrected more easily:

Programming errors are often called "bugs" and the process of tracking them down is often called "debugging".

- **Syntax Error** – occurs when the interpreter encounters code that does not conform to the Python language rules. For example, a missing quote mark around a string. The interpreter halts and reports the error without executing the program.

- **Runtime Error** – occurs during execution of the program, at the time when the program runs. For example, when a variable name is later mis-typed so the variable cannot be recognized. The interpreter runs the program but halts at the error and reports the nature of the error as an "Exception".

- **Semantic Error** – occurs when the program performs unexpectedly. For example, when order precedence has not been specified in an expression. The interpreter runs the program and does not report an error.

Correcting syntax and runtime errors is fairly straightforward, as the interpreter reports where the error occurred or the nature of the error type, but semantic errors require code examination.

syntax.py

1. Launch a plain text editor then add a statement to output a string that omits a closing quote mark
print('Python in easy steps)

2. Save the file in your scripts directory then open a Command Prompt window there and run this program – to see the interpreter report the syntax error and indicate the position in the code where the error occurs

Beware

Typically, the syntax error indicator points to the next character after an omission in the code.

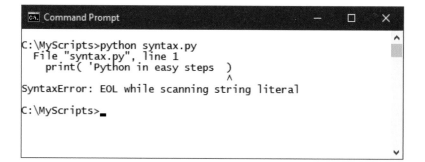

```
C:\MyScripts>python syntax.py
  File "syntax.py", line 1
    print( 'Python in easy steps  )
                                  ^
SyntaxError: EOL while scanning string literal

C:\MyScripts>_
```

3   Insert a quote mark before the closing parenthesis to terminate the string, then save the file and run the program again – to see the error has been corrected

4   Next, begin a new program by initializing a variable, then try to output its value with an incorrect variable name – to see the interpreter report a runtime error

     title = 'Python in easy steps'
     print(titel)

runtime.py

```
C:\MyScripts>python runtime.py
Traceback (most recent call last):
  File "runtime.py", line 2, in <module>
    print( titel )
NameError: name 'titel' is not defined

C:\MyScripts>_
```

Details of how to handle runtime Exception errors in your script code are provided on page 74.

5   Amend the variable name to match that in the variable declaration, then save the file and run the program again – to see the error has been corrected

6   Now, begin a new program by initializing a variable, then try to output an expression using its value without explicit precedence – to see a possibly unexpected result of 28

     num = 3
     print(num * 8 + 4)

semantic.py

```
C:\MyScripts>python semantic.py
28

C:\MyScripts>_
```

7   Add parentheses to group the expression as **3 * (8 + 4)**, then save the file and run the program again – to see the expected result of 36, correcting the semantic error

Summary

- Python is a high-level programming language that is processed by the Python interpreter to produce results.

- Python uses indentation to group statements into code blocks, where other languages use keywords or punctuation.

- Python 2.7 is the final version of the 2.x branch of development, but the 3.x branch has the latest improvements.

- Windows users can install Python with an installer, and Linux users can install Python with their package manager.

- The Python interpreter has an interactive mode where you can test snippets of code and is useful for debugging code.

- A Python program is simply a text file created with a plain text editor and saved with a ".py" file extension.

- The Python **print()** function outputs the string specified within its parentheses.

- String values must be enclosed between quote marks.

- Where multiple versions of Python are installed on the same system it is important to explicitly call the desired interpreter.

- A Python variable is a named container whose stored value can be referenced via that variable's name.

- A Python variable can contain any data type but must be given an initial value when it is declared.

- The Python **input()** function outputs the string specified within its parentheses, then waits to read a line of input.

- Syntax errors due to incorrect code are recognized by the interpreter before execution of the program.

- Runtime errors due to exceptions are recognized by the interpreter during execution of the program.

- Semantic errors due to unexpected performance are not recognized by the interpreter.

2

Performing operations

This chapter introduces the Python operators, and demonstrates the operations they can perform.

Doing arithmetic

The arithmetical operators commonly used in Python programming are listed in the table below, together with the operation they perform:

Operator:	Operation:
+	Addition
-	Subtraction
*	Multiplication
/	Division
%	Modulo
//	Floor division
**	Exponent

The operators for addition, subtraction, multiplication, and division act as you would expect. Care must be taken, however, to group expressions where more than one operator is used to clarify the expression – operations within innermost parentheses are performed first. For example, with this expression:

a = b * c - d % e / f

The desired order in which the operations should be performed is unclear but can be clarified by adding parentheses, like this:

a = (b * c) - ((d % e) / f)

The **%** modulo operator will divide the first given number by the second given number and return the remainder of the operation. This is useful to determine if a number has an odd or even value.

The **//** floor division operator performs just like the **/** division operator, but truncates the result at the decimal point – removing any floating point value.

The ****** exponent operator returns the result of the first operand raised to the power of the second operand.

Hot tip

Values used with operators to form expressions are called "operands" – in the expression **2 + 3** the numerical values **2** and **3** are the operands.

...cont'd

1 Start a new Python script by initializing two variables with integer values

```
a = 8
b = 2
```

arithmetic.py

2 Next, display the result of adding the variable values

```
print( 'Addition:\t' , a , '+' , b , '=' , a + b )
```

3 Now, display the result of subtracting the variable values

```
print( 'Subtraction:\t' , a , '-' , b , '=' , a - b )
```

Hot tip

The **\t** escape sequence shown here adds an invisible tab character to format the output.

4 Then, display the result of multiplying the variable values

```
print( 'Multiplication:\t' , a , 'x' , b , '=' , a * b )
```

5 Display the result of dividing the variable values both with and without the floating-point value

```
print( 'Division:\t' , a , '÷' , b , '=' , a / b )
print( 'Floor Division:\t' , a , '÷' , b , '=' , a // b )
```

6 Next, display the remainder after dividing the values

```
print( 'Modulo:\t' , a , '%' , b , '=' , a % b )
```

7 Finally, display the result of raising the first operand to the power of the second operand

```
print( 'Exponent:\t ' , a , '² = ' , a ** b , sep = '' )
```

8 Save the file in your scripts directory, then open a Command Prompt window there and run this program – to see the result of the arithmetical operations

Don't forget

You can use the **sep** parameter to explicitly specify the separation between output – here it specifies no spaces by assigning two unspaced single quote marks.

```
C:\MyScripts>python arithmetic.py
Addition:        8 + 2 = 10
Subtraction:     8 - 2 = 6
Multiplication:  8 x 2 = 16
Division:        8 ÷ 2 = 4.0
Floor Division:  8 ÷ 2 = 4
Modulus:         8 % 2 = 0
Exponent:        8² = 64

C:\MyScripts>_
```

Assigning values

The operators that are used in Python programming to assign values are listed in the table below. All except the simple = assignment operator are a shorthand form of a longer expression, so each equivalent is given for clarity:

Operator:	Example:	Equivalent:
=	a = b	a = b
+=	a += b	a = (a + b)
-=	a -= b	a = (a - b)
*=	a *= b	a = (a * b)
/=	a /= b	a = (a / b)
%=	a %= b	a = (a % b)
//=	a //= b	a = (a // b)
**=	a **= b	a = (a ** b)

In the example above, the variable named "a" is assigned the value that is contained in the variable named "b" – so that becomes the new value stored in the **a** variable.

The += operator is useful to add a value onto an existing value that is stored in the **a** variable.

In the table example, the += operator first adds the value contained in variable **a** to the value contained in variable **b**. It then assigns the result to become the new value stored in variable **a**.

All the other operators work in the same way by making the arithmetical operation between the two values first, then assigning the result of that operation to the first variable – to become its new stored value.

With the %= operator, the first operand **a** is divided by the second operand **b**, then the remainder of that operation is assigned to the **a** variable.

Don't forget

It is important to regard the = operator to mean "assign" rather than "equals" to avoid confusion with the == equality operator.

Start a new Python script that initializes two variables by assigning integer values and displays both assigned values

```
a = 8
b = 4
print( 'Assign Values:\t\t' , 'a =' , a , '\tb =' , b )
```

assign.py

 Next, add and assign a new value to the first variable and display its stored value

```
a += b
print( 'Add & Assign:\t\t' ,'a =' , a , '(8 + 4)' )
```

3 Now, subtract and assign a new value to the first variable and display its stored value, then multiply and assign a value to the first variable and display its stored value

```
a -= b
print( 'Subtract & Assign:\t' , 'a =' , a , ' (12 - 4)' )

a *= b
print( 'Multiply & Assign:\t' , 'a =' , a , '(8 x 4)' )
```

4 Finally, divide and assign a new value to the first variable and display its stored value, then modulo and assign a value to the first variable and display its stored value

```
a /= b
print( 'Divide & Assign:\t' , 'a =' , a , '(32 ÷ 4)' )

a %= b
print( 'Modulo & Assign:\t' , 'a =' , a , '(8 % 4)' )
```

 Save the file in your scripts directory, then open a Command Prompt window there and run this program – to see the result of the assignment operations

```
C:\MyScripts>python assign.py
Assign Values:          a = 8   b = 4
Add & Assign:           a = 12 (8 + 4)
Subtract & Assign:      a = 8  (12 - 4)
Multiply & Assign:      a = 32 (8 x 4)
Divide & Assign:        a = 8.0 (32 ÷ 4)
Modulus & Assign:       a = 0.0 (8 % 4)

C:\MyScripts>
```

Beware

Unlike the = assign operator, the == equality operator compares operands and is described on page 30.

Comparing values

The operators that are commonly used in Python programming to compare two operand values are listed in the table below:

Operator:	Comparative test:
==	Equality
!=	Inequality
>	Greater than
<	Less than
>=	Greater than or equal to
<=	Less than or equal to

The == equality operator compares two operands and will return **True** if both are equal in value, otherwise it will return a **False** value. If both are the same number they are equal, or if both are characters their ASCII code values are compared numerically to achieve the comparison result.

Conversely, the != inequality operator returns **True** if two operands are not equal, using the same rules as the == equality operator, otherwise it returns **False**. Equality and inequality operators are useful in testing the state of two variables to perform conditional branching in a program according to the result.

The > "greater than" operator compares two operands and will return **True** if the first is greater in value than the second, or it will return **False** if it is equal or less in value. The < "less than" operator makes the same comparison but returns **True** if the first operand is less in value than the second, otherwise it returns **False**. A > "greater than" or < "less than" operator is often used to test the value of an iteration counter in a loop.

Adding the = operator after a > "greater than" or < "less than" operator makes it also return **True** if the two operands are exactly equal in value.

Hot tip

A-Z uppercase characters have ASCII code values 65-90 and a-z lowercase characters have ASCII code values 97-122.

30

1 Start a new Python script by initializing five variables with values for comparison
```
nil = 0
num = 0
max = 1
cap = 'A'
low = 'a'
```

comparison.py

2 Next, add statements to display the results of numeric and character equality comparisons
```
print( 'Equality :\t' , nil , '==' , num , nil == num )
print( 'Equality :\t' , cap , '==' , low , cap == low )
```

The \t escape sequence shown here adds an invisible tab character to format the output.

3 Now, add a statement to display the result of an inequality comparison
```
print( 'Inequality :\t' , nil , '!=' , max , nil != max )
```

4 Then, add statements to display the results of greater and lesser comparisons
```
print( 'Greater :\t' , nil , '>' , max , nil > max )
print( 'Lesser :\t' , nil , '<' , max , nil < max )
```

5 Finally, add statements to display the results of greater or equal and lesser or equal comparisons
```
print( 'More Or Equal :\t' , nil , '>=' , num , nil >= num )
print( 'Less or Equal :\t' , max , '<=' , num , max <= num )
```

6 Save the file in your scripts directory, then open a Command Prompt window there and run this program – to see the result of comparison operations

The ASCII code value for uppercase "A" is 65, but for lowercase "a" it's 97 – so their comparison here returns **False**.

```
Command Prompt                                      —  □  ×

C:\MyScripts>python comparison.py
Equality :          0 == 0 True
Equality :          A == a False
Inequality :        0 != 1 True
Greater :           0 > 1 False
Lesser :            0 < 1 True
More Or Equal :     0 >= 0 True
Less or Equal :     1 <= 0 False

C:\MyScripts>_
```

Assessing logic

The logical operators most commonly used in Python programming are listed in the table below:

Operator:	Operation:
and	Logical AND
or	Logical OR
not	Logical NOT

The term "Boolean" refers to a system of logical thought developed by the English mathematician George Boole (1815-1864).

The logical operators are used with operands that have Boolean values of **True** or **False**, or are values that convert to **True** or **False**.

The (logical AND) **and** operator will evaluate two operands and return **True** only if both operands themselves are **True**. Otherwise the **and** operator will return **False**. This is used in conditional branching where the direction of a program is determined by testing two conditions – if both conditions are satisfied, the program will go in a certain direction, otherwise it will take a different direction.

Unlike the **and** operator that needs both operands to be **True**, the (logical OR) **or** operator will evaluate its two operands and return **True** if either one of the operands itself returns **True**. If neither operand returns **True**, then the **or** operator will return **False**. This is useful in Python programming to perform a certain action if either one of two test conditions has been met.

The (logical NOT) **not** operator is a unary operator that is used before a single operand. It returns the inverse value of the given operand, so if the variable **a** had a value of **True** then **not a** would have a value of **False**. The **not** operator is useful in Python programs to toggle the value of a variable in successive loop iterations with a statement like **a = not a**. This ensures that on each iteration of the loop, the Boolean value is reversed, like flicking a light switch on and off.

1 Start a new Python script by initializing two variables with Boolean values for logical evaluation

```
a = True
b = False
```

logic.py

2 Next, add statements to display the results of logical AND evaluations

```
print( 'AND Logic:' )
print( 'a and a =' , a and a )
print( 'a and b =' , a and b )
print( 'b and b =' , b and b )
```

3 Now, add statements to display the results of logical OR evaluations

```
print( '\nOR Logic:' )
print( 'a or a =' , a or a )
print( 'a or b =' , a or b )
print( 'b or b =' , b or b )
```

Hot tip

In Python programming, Boolean values can also be represented numerically where **True** is **1** and **False** is **0** (zero).

4 Finally, add statements to display the results of logical NOT evaluations

```
print( '\nNOT Logic:' )
print( 'a =' , a , '\tnot a =' , not a )
print( 'b =' , b , '\tnot b =' , not b )
```

5 Save the file in your scripts directory, then open a Command Prompt window there and run this program – to see the result of logic operations

```
C:\MyScripts>python logic.py
AND Logic:
a and a = True
a and b = False
b and b = False

OR Logic:
a or a = True
a or b = True
b or b = False

NOT Logic:
a = True        not a = False
b = False       not b = True

C:\MyScripts>_
```

Don't forget

Note that the expression **False and False** returns **False**, not **True** – perhaps demonstrating the maxim "two wrongs don't make a right".

Examining conditions

Many programming languages, such as C++ or Java, have a **?:** "ternary" operator that evaluates an expression for a **True** or **False** condition then returns one of two specified values depending on the result of the evaluation. A **?:** ternary operator has this syntax:

(*test-expression*) **?** *if-true-return-this* **:** *if-false-return-this*

Unlike other programming languages, Python does not have a **?:** ternary operator but has instead a "conditional expression" that works in a similar way using **if** and **else** keywords with this syntax:

if-true-return-this **if** (*test-expression*) **else** *if-false-return-this*

Although the conditional expression syntax can initially appear confusing, it is well worth becoming familiar with this expression as it can execute powerful program branching with minimal code. For example, to branch when a variable is not a value of one:

if-true-do-this **if** (var != 1) **else** *if-false-do-this*

The conditional expression can be used in Python programming to assign the maximum or minimum value of two variables to a third variable. For example, to assign a minimum like this:

c = a if (a < b) else b

The expression in parentheses returns **True** when the value of variable **a** is less than that of variable **b** – so in this case the lesser value of variable **a** gets assigned to variable **c**.

Similarly, replacing the **<** less than operator in the test expression with the **>** greater than operator would assign the greater value of variable **b** to variable **c**.

Another common use of the conditional expression incorporates the **%** modulo operator in the test expression to determine if the value of a variable is an odd number or an even number:

if-true(odd)-do-this **if** (var % 2 != 0) **else** *if-false(even)-do-this*

Where the result of dividing the variable value by two does leave a remainder, the number is odd – where there is no remainder, the number is even. The test expression (**var % 2 == 1**) would have the same effect but it is preferable to test for inequality – it's easier to spot when something is different than when it's identical.

1 Start a new Python script by initializing two variables with integer values for conditional evaluation
```
a = 1
b = 2
```

PY

condition.py

2 Next, add statements to display the results of conditional evaluation – describing the first variable's value
```
print( '\nVariable a Is :' , 'One' if ( a == 1 ) else 'Not One' )
print( 'Variable a Is :' , 'Even' if ( a % 2 == 0 ) else 'Odd' )
```

← conditional expressions

3 Now, add statements to display the results of conditional evaluation – describing the second variable's value
```
print( '\nVariable b Is :' , 'One' if ( b == 1 ) else 'Not One' )
print( 'Variable b Is :' , 'Even' if ( b % 2 == 0 ) else 'Odd' )
```

4 Then, add a statement to assign the result of a conditional evaluation to a new variable
```
max = a if ( a > b ) else b
```

5 Finally, add a statement to display the assigned result – identifying the greater of the two variable values
```
print( '\nGreater Value Is:' , max )
```

6 Save the file in your scripts directory, then open a Command Prompt window there and run this program – to see the result of conditional expression operations

```
Command Prompt                           —   □   ×

C:\MyScripts>python condition.py

Variable a Is : One
Variable a Is : Odd

Variable b Is : Not One
Variable b Is : Even

Greater Value Is: 2

C:\MyScripts>_
```

Beware

You may find that some Python programmers dislike conditional expressions as they consider their syntax contradicts the principle of easy readability.

Setting precedence

Operator precedence determines the order in which the Python interpreter evaluates expressions. For example, in the expression **3 * 8 + 4** the default order of precedence determines that multiplication is completed first, so the result is 28 (24 + 4).

The table below lists operator precedence in descending order – those on the top row have highest precedence, those on lower rows have successively lower precedence. The precedence of operators on the same row is chained Left-To-Right:

Don't forget

The * multiply operator is on a higher row than the + addition operator – so in the expression **3 * 8 + 4** multiplication is completed first, before the addition.

36

Hot tip

The bitwise, identity, and membership operators are introduced later in this book – but are included here for completeness.

Operator:	Description:
**	Exponent
+ - ~	Positive Negative Bitwise NOT
* / // %	Multiplication Division Floor division Modulo
+ -	Addition Subtraction
|	Bitwise OR
^	Bitwise XOR
&	Bitwise AND
>> <<	Bitwise right shift Bitwise left shift
>, >=, <, <=, ==, !=	Comparison
= , %= , /= , //= , -= , += , *= , **=	Assignment
is , is not	Identity
in , not in	Membership
not	Boolean NOT
and	Boolean AND
or	Boolean OR

...cont'd

1 Start a new Python script by initializing three variables with integer values for precedence comparison
```
a = 2
b = 4
c = 8
```

precedence.py

2 Next, add statements to display the results of default precedence and forcing addition before multiplication
```
print( '\nDefault Order:\t', a, '*', c,'+', b, '=', a * c + b )
print( 'Forced Order:\t', a, '* (', c,'+', b, ') =', a * ( c + b ) )
```

3 Now, add statements to display the results of default precedence and forcing subtraction before division
```
print( '\nDefault Order:\t', c, '//', b, '-', a, '=', c // b - a )
print( 'Forced Order:\t', c, '// (', b,'-', a, ') =', c // ( b - a ) )
```

The // floor division operator truncates floating point values at the decimal point – but the / division operator retains them.

4 Finally, add statements to display the results of default precedence and forcing addition before modulo operation and before exponent operation
```
print( '\nDefault Order:\t', c, '%', a, '+', b, '=', c % a + b )
print( 'Forced Order:\t', c, '% (', a, '+', b, ') =', c % ( a + b ) )

print( '\nDefault Order:\t', c, '**', a, '+', b, '=', c ** a + b )
print( 'Forced Order:\t', c, '** (', a, '+', b, ') =', c ** ( a + b ) )
```

37

5 Save the file in your scripts directory, then open a Command Prompt window there and run this program – to see the results of default and explicit precedence

```
Command Prompt                                    —   □   ×

C:\MyScripts>python precedence.py

Default Order:    2 * 8 + 4 = 20
Forced Order:     2 * ( 8 + 4 ) = 24

Default Order:    8 // 4 - 2 = 0
Forced Order:     8 // ( 4 - 2 ) = 4

Default Order:    8 % 2 + 4 = 4
Forced Order:     8 % ( 2 + 4 ) = 2

Default Order:    8 ** 2 + 4 = 68
Forced Order:     8 ** ( 2 + 4 ) = 262144

C:\MyScripts>
```

Do not rely upon default precedence – always use parentheses to clarify your expressions.

Casting data types

Although Python variables can store data of any data type, it is important to recognize the different types of data they contain to avoid errors when manipulating that data in a program. There are several Python data types but by far the most common ones are **str** (string), **int** (integer), and **float** (floating-point).

Data type recognition is especially important when assigning numeric data to variables from user input as it is stored by default as a **str** (string) data type. String values cannot be used for arithmetical expressions as attempting to add string values together simply concatenates (joins) the values together rather than adding them numerically. For example '8' + '4' = '84'.

Fortunately, the data type of stored values can be easily converted ("cast") into a different data type using built-in Python functions. The value to be converted is specified within the parentheses that follow the function name. Casting **str** (string) values to become **int** (integer) values allows them to be used for arithmetical expressions, for example, 8 + 4 = 12.

Python's built-in data type conversion functions return a new object representing the converted value, and those conversion functions most frequently used are listed in the table below:

Beware

Converting a **float** (floating-point) data type to an **int** (integer) data type will truncate the number at the decimal point losing the fraction.

Function:	Description:
int(*x*)	Converts *x* to an integer whole number
float(*x*)	Converts *x* to a floating-point number
str(*x*)	Converts *x* to a string representation
chr(*x*)	Converts integer *x* to a character
unichr(*x*)	Converts integer *x* to a Unicode character
ord(*x*)	Converts character *x* to its integer value
hex(*x*)	Converts integer *x* to a hexadecimal string
oct(*x*)	Converts integer *x* to an octal string

The Python built-in **type()** function can be used to determine to which data type class the value contained in a variable belongs, simply by specifying that variable's name within its parentheses.

① Start a new Python script by initializing two variables with numeric values from user input

```
a = input( 'Enter A Number: ' )
b = input( 'Now Enter Another Number: ' )
```

cast.py

② Next, add statements to add the variable values together then display the combined result and its data type – to see a concatenated string value result

```
sum = a + b
print( '\nData Type sum :' , sum , type( sum ) )
```

③ Now, add statements to add cast variable values together then display the result and its data type – to see a total integer value result

```
sum = int( a ) + int( b )
print( 'Data Type sum :' , sum , type( sum ) )
```

④ Then, add statements to cast a variable value then display the result and its data type – to see a total float value

```
sum = float( sum )
print( 'Data Type sum :' , sum , type( sum ) )
```

⑤ Finally, add statements to cast an integer representation of a variable value then display the result and its data type – to see a character string value

```
sum = chr( int( sum ) )
print( 'Data Type sum :' , sum , type( sum ) )
```

⑥ Save the file in your scripts directory, then open a Command Prompt window there and run this program – to see the result of casting as various data types

The number 65 is the ASCII character code for uppercase letter A.

```
Command Prompt                              —    □    X

C:\MyScripts>python cast.py
Enter A Number: 60
Now Enter Another Number: 5

Data Type sum : 605 <class 'str'>
Data Type sum : 65 <class 'int'>
Data Type sum : 65.0 <class 'float'>
Data Type sum : A <class 'str'>

C:\MyScripts>_
```

Manipulating bits

In computer terms, each byte comprises eight bits that can each contain a **1** or a **0** to store a binary number, representing decimal values from 0 to 255. Each bit contributes a decimal component only when that bit contains a **1**. Components are designated right-to-left from the "Least Significant Bit" (LSB) to the "Most Significant Bit" (MSB). The binary number in the bit pattern below is **00110010** and represents the decimal number 50 (2+16+32):

Bit No.	8 MSB	7	6	5	4	3	2	1 LSB
Decimal	128	64	32	16	8	4	2	1
Binary	0	0	1	1	0	0	1	0

It is possible to manipulate individual parts of a byte using the Python "bitwise" operators listed and described below:

Operator:	Name:	Binary number operation:
|	OR	Return a **1** in each bit where either of two compared bits is a **1** Example: **1010 | 0101 = 1111**
&	AND	Return a **1** in each bit where both of two compared bits is a **1** Example: **1010 && 1100 = 1000**
~	NOT	Return a **1** in each bit where neither of two compared bits is a **1** Example: **1010 ~ 0011 = 0100**
^	XOR	Return a **1** in each bit where only one of two compared bits is a **1** Example: **1010 ^ 0100 = 1110**
<<	Shift left	Move each bit that is a **1** a specified number of bits to the left Example: **0010 << 2 = 1000**
>>	Shift right	Move each bit that is a **1** a specified number of bits to the right Example: **1000 >> 2 = 0010**

Don't forget

Many Python programmers never use bitwise operators but it is useful to understand what they are and how they may be used.

Hot tip

Each half of a byte is known as a "nibble" (4 bits). The binary numbers in the examples in the table describe values stored in a nibble.

Unless programming for a device with limited resources there is seldom a need to utilize bitwise operators, but they can be useful. For instance, the XOR (eXclusive OR) operator lets you exchange values between two variables without the need for a third variable.

bitwise.py

1. Start a new Python script by initializing two variables with numeric values and display these initial values
```
a = 10
b = 5
print( 'a =' , a , '\tb = ' , b )
```

2. Next, add a statement to change the first variable's decimal value by binary bit manipulation
```
# 1010 ^ 0101 = 1111 (decimal 15)
a = a ^ b
```

3. Now, add a statement to change the second variable's decimal value by binary bit manipulation
```
# 1111 ^ 0101 = 1010 (decimal 10)
b = a ^ b
```

4. Then, add a statement to change the first variable's decimal value once more by further bit manipulation
```
# 1111 ^ 1010 = 0101 (decimal 5)
a = a ^ b
```

5. Finally, add a statement to display the exchanged values
```
print( 'a =' , a , '\tb = ' , b )
```

6. Save the file in your scripts directory, then open a Command Prompt window there and run this program – to see the result of bitwise operations

```
C:\MyScripts>python bitwise.py
a = 10   b =   5
a = 5    b =   10

C:\MyScripts>
```

Beware

Do not confuse bitwise operators with logical operators. Bitwise operators compare binary numbers, whereas logical operators evaluate Boolean values.

Summary

- Arithmetical operators can form expressions with two operands for addition **+**, subtraction **-**, multiplication *****, division **/**, floor division **//**, modulo **%,** or exponent ******.

- The assignment **=** operator can be combined with an arithmetical operator to perform an arithmetical calculation then assign its result.

- Comparison operators can form expressions comparing two operands for equality **==**, inequality **!=**, greater **>**, lesser **<**, greater or equal **>=**, and lesser or equal **<=** values.

- Logical **and** and **or** operators form expressions evaluating two operands to return a Boolean value of **True** or **False**.

- The logical **not** operator returns the inverse Boolean value of a single operand.

- A conditional **if-else** expression evaluates a given expression for a Boolean **True** or **False** value, then returns one of two operands depending on its result.

- Expressions containing multiple operators will execute their operations in accordance with the default precedence rules unless explicitly determined by the addition of parentheses **( )**.

- The data type of a variable value can be converted to a different data type by the built-in Python functions **int()**, **float()**, and **str()** to return a new converted object.

- Python's built-in **type()** function determines to which data type class a specified variable belongs.

- Bitwise operators OR **|**, AND **&**, NOT **~**, and XOR **^** each return a value after comparison of the values within two bits, whereas the Shift left **<<** and Shift right **>>** operators move the bit values a specified number of bits in their direction.

3 Making statements

This chapter demonstrates how statements can evaluate expressions to determine the direction in which a Python program proceeds.

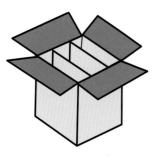

Writing lists

In Python programming, a variable must be assigned an initial value (initialized) in the statement that declares it in a program, otherwise the interpreter will report a "not defined" error.

Multiple variables can be initialized with a common value in a single statement using a sequence of = assignments. For example, to simultaneously assign a common value to three variables:

a = b = c = 10

Alternatively, multiple variables can be initialized with differing values in a single statement using comma separators. For example, to simultaneously assign different values to three variables:

a , b , c = 1 , 2 , 3

Unlike regular variables, which can only store a single item of data, a Python "list" is a variable that can store multiple items of data. The data is stored sequentially in list "elements" that are index numbered starting at zero. So the first value is stored in element zero, the second value is stored in element one, and so on.

A list is created much like any other variable, but is initialized by assigning values as a comma-separated list between square brackets. For example, creating a list named "nums", like this:

nums = [0 , 1 , 2 , 3 , 4 , 5]

An individual list element can be referenced using the list name followed by square brackets containing that element's index number. This means that **nums[1]** references the second element in the example above – not the first element, as element numbering starts at zero.

Lists can have more than one index – to represent multiple dimensions, rather than the single dimension of a regular list. Multi-dimensional lists of three indices and more are uncommon, but two-dimensional lists are useful to store grid-based information such as X,Y coordinates.

A list of string values can even be considered to be a multi-dimensional list, as each string is itself a list of characters. So each character can be referenced by its index number within its particular string.

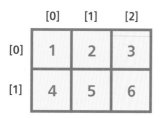

...cont'd

1 Start a new Python script by initializing a list of three elements containing string values
quarter = ['January' , 'February' , 'March']

list.py

2 Next, add statements to individually display the value contained in each list element
print('First Month :' , quarter[0])
print('Second Month :' , quarter[1])
print('Third Month :' , quarter[2])

Hot tip

3 Add a statement to create a multi-dimensional list of two elements, which themselves are lists that each have three elements containing integer values
coords = [[1 , 2 , 3] , [4 , 5 , 6]]

String indices may also be negative numbers – to start counting from the right where -1 references the last letter.

4 Now, add statements to display the values contained in two specific inner list elements
print('\nTop Left 0,0 :' , coords[0][0])
print('Bottom Right 1,2 :' , coords[1][2])

5 Finally, add a statement to display just one character of a string value
print('\nSecond Month First Letter :' , quarter[1][0])

45

6 Save the file in your scripts directory, then open a Command Prompt window there and run this program – to see the list element values get displayed

Don't forget

```
Command Prompt                          —  □  ×

C:\MyScripts>python list.py
First Month : January
Second Month : February
Third Month : March

Top Left 0,0 : 1
Bottom Right 1,2 : 6

Second Month First Letter : F

C:\MyScripts>_
```

Loop structures, which are introduced later in this chapter, are often used to iterate through list elements.

Manipulating lists

List variables, which can contain multiple items of data, are widely used in Python programming and have a number of "methods" that can be "dot-suffixed" to the list name for manipulation:

List Method:	Description:
list.**append(x)**	Adds item *x* to the end of the list
list.**extend(L)**	Adds all items in list *L* to the end of the list
list.**insert(i,x)**	Inserts item *x* at index position *i*
list.**remove(x)**	Removes first item *x* from the list
list.**pop(i)**	Removes item at index position *i* and returns it
list.**index(x)**	Returns the index position in the list of first item *x*
list.**count(x)**	Returns the number of times *x* appears in the list
list.**sort()**	Sort all list items, in place
list.**reverse()**	Reverse all list items, in place

Hot tip

For lists that contain both numerical and string values, the **sort()** method returns the list elements sorted first numerically then alphabetically – for example as 1,2,3,A,B,C.

Python also has a useful **len(L)** function that returns the length of the list **L** as the total number of elements it contains. Like the **index()** and **count()** methods, the returned value is numeric so cannot be directly concatenated to a text string for output.

String representation of numeric values can, however, be produced by Python's **str(n)** function for concatenation to other strings, which returns a string version of the numeric **n** value. Similarly, a string representation of an entire list can be returned by the **str(L)** function for concatenation to other strings. In both cases, remember that the original version remains unchanged as the returned versions are merely copies of the original version.

Hot tip

Python also has an **int(s)** function that returns a numeric version of the string **s** value.

Individual list elements can be deleted by specifying their index number to the Python **del(i)** function. This can remove a single element at a specified *i* index position, or a "slice" of elements can be removed using slice notation *i1:i2* to specify the index number of the first and last element. In this case, *i1* is the index number of the first element to be removed and all elements up to, but not including, the element at the *i2* index number will be removed.

...cont'd

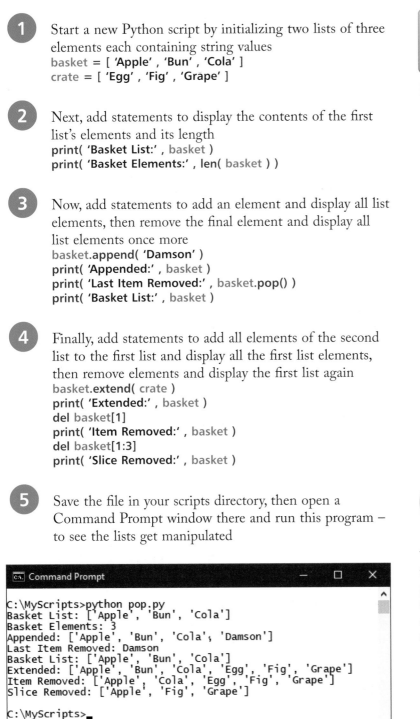

1 Start a new Python script by initializing two lists of three elements each containing string values
```
basket = [ 'Apple' , 'Bun' , 'Cola' ]
crate = [ 'Egg' , 'Fig' , 'Grape' ]
```

pop.py

2 Next, add statements to display the contents of the first list's elements and its length
```
print( 'Basket List:' , basket )
print( 'Basket Elements:' , len( basket ) )
```

3 Now, add statements to add an element and display all list elements, then remove the final element and display all list elements once more
```
basket.append( 'Damson' )
print( 'Appended:' , basket )
print( 'Last Item Removed:' , basket.pop() )
print( 'Basket List:' , basket )
```

4 Finally, add statements to add all elements of the second list to the first list and display all the first list elements, then remove elements and display the first list again
```
basket.extend( crate )
print( 'Extended:' , basket )
del basket[1]
print( 'Item Removed:' , basket )
del basket[1:3]
print( 'Slice Removed:' , basket )
```

5 Save the file in your scripts directory, then open a Command Prompt window there and run this program – to see the lists get manipulated

```
C:\MyScripts>python pop.py
Basket List: ['Apple', 'Bun', 'Cola']
Basket Elements: 3
Appended: ['Apple', 'Bun', 'Cola', 'Damson']
Last Item Removed: Damson
Basket List: ['Apple', 'Bun', 'Cola']
Extended: ['Apple', 'Bun', 'Cola', 'Egg', 'Fig', 'Grape']
Item Removed: ['Apple', 'Cola', 'Egg', 'Fig', 'Grape']
Slice Removed: ['Apple', 'Fig', 'Grape']

C:\MyScripts>_
```

The last index number in the slice denotes at what point to stop removing elements, but the element at that position does not get removed.

Restricting lists

Tuple

The values in a regular list can be changed as the program proceeds (they are "mutable"), but a list can be created with fixed "immutable" values that cannot be changed by the program. A restrictive immutable Python list is known as a "tuple" and is created by assigning values as a comma-separated list between parentheses in a process known as "tuple packing":

colors-tuple = ('Red' , 'Green' , 'Red' , 'Blue', 'Red')

An individual tuple element can be referenced using the tuple name followed by square brackets containing that element's index number. Usefully, all values stored inside a tuple can be assigned to individual variables in a process known as "sequence unpacking":

a , b , c , d , e = colors-tuple

Set

The values in a regular list can be repeated in its elements, as in the tuple above, but a list of unique values can be created where duplication is not allowed. A restrictive Python list of unique values is known as a "set" and is created by assigning values as a comma-separated list between curly brackets (braces):

phonetic-set = { 'Alpha' , 'Bravo' , 'Charlie' }

Individual set elements cannot be referenced using the set name followed by square brackets containing an index number, but instead sets have methods that can be dot-suffixed to the set name for manipulation and comparison:

Set Method:	Description:
set.add(*x*)	Adds item *x* to the set
set.update(*x,y,z*)	Adds multiple items to the set
set.copy()	Returns a copy of the set
set.pop()	Removes one random item from the set
set.discard(*x*)	Removes item *x* if found in the set
set1.intersection(*set2*)	Returns items that appear in both sets
set1.difference(*set2*)	Returns items in *set1* but not in *set2*

Don't forget

Like index numbering with lists, the items in a tuple sequence are numbered from zero.

Beware

There must be the same number of variables as items to unpack a tuple.

Hot tip

More set methods can be found in the Python documentation.

48

...cont'd

The Python **type()** function can be used to ascertain these lists' data structure class, and the Python built-in membership operator **in** can be used to find values in a set.

1 Start a new Python script by initializing a tuple then display its contents, length, and type
```
zoo = ( 'Kangaroo' , 'Leopard' , 'Moose' )
print( 'Tuple:' , zoo , '\tLength:' , len( zoo ) )
print( type( zoo ) )
```

set.py

2 Next, initialize a set and add another element, then display its contents, length, and type
```
bag = { 'Red' , 'Green' , 'Blue' }
bag.add( 'Yellow' )
print( '\nSet:' , bag , '\tLength' , len( bag ) )
print( type( bag ) )
```

3 Now, add statements to seek two values in the set
```
print( '\nIs Green In bag Set?:' , 'Green' in bag )
print( 'Is Orange In bag Set?:' , 'Orange' in bag )
```

4 Finally, initialize a second set and display its contents, length, and all common values found in both sets
```
box = { 'Red' , 'Purple' , 'Yellow' }
print( '\nSet:' , box , '\t\tLength' , len( box ) )
print( 'Common To Both Sets:' , bag.intersection( box ) )
```

5 Save the file in your scripts directory, then open a Command Prompt window there and run this program – to see the tuple and set values

```
C:\MyScripts>python set.py
Tuple: ('Kangaroo', 'Leopard', 'Moose')          Length: 3
<class 'tuple'>

Set: {'Blue', 'Green', 'Yellow', 'Red'}          Length 4
<class 'set'>

Is Green In bag Set?: True
Is Orange In bag Set?: False

Set: {'Purple', 'Yellow', 'Red'}                 Length 3
Common To Both Sets: {'Red', 'Yellow'}

C:\MyScripts>_
```

A set may also be created by specifying the brace-enclosed list within the parentheses of a **set()** constructor and an immutable set can be created using a **frozenset()** constructor.

Associating list elements

In Python programming a "dictionary" is a data container that can store multiple items of data as a list of key:value pairs. Unlike regular list container values, which are referenced by their index number, values stored in dictionaries are referenced by their associated key. The key must be unique within that dictionary, and is typically a string name although numbers may be used.

Creating a dictionary is simply a matter of assigning the key:value pairs as a comma-separated list between curly brackets (braces) to a name of your choice. Strings must be enclosed within quotes, as usual, and a : colon character must come between the key and its associated value.

A key:value pair can be deleted from a dictionary by specifying the dictionary name and the pair's key to the **del** keyword. Conversely, a key:value pair can be added to a dictionary by assigning a value to the dictionary's name and a new key.

Python dictionaries have a **keys()** method that can be dot-suffixed to the dictionary name to return a list, in random order, of all the keys in that dictionary. If you prefer the keys to be sorted into alphanumeric order, simply enclose the statement within the parentheses of the Python **sorted()** function.

A dictionary can be searched to see if it contains a particular key with the Python **in** operator, using the syntax *key* **in** *dictionary*. The search will return a Boolean **True** value when the key is found in the specified dictionary, otherwise it will return **False**.

Dictionaries are the final type of data container available in Python programming. In summary, the various types are:

- **Variable** – stores a single value.

- **List** – stores multiple values in an ordered index.

- **Tuple** – stores multiple fixed values in a sequence.

- **Set** – stores multiple unique values in an unordered collection.

- **Dictionary** – stores multiple unordered key:value pairs.

In other programming languages a list is often called an "array" and a dictionary is often called an "associative array".

Data is frequently associated as key:value pairs – for example, when you submit a web form, a text value typed into an input field is typically associated with that text field's name as its key.

...cont'd

dict.py

1 Start a new Python script by initializing a dictionary then display its key:value contents
```
dict = { 'name' : 'Bob' , 'ref' : 'Python' , 'sys' : 'Win' }
print( 'Dictionary:' , dict )
```

2 Next, display a single value referenced by its key
```
print( '\nReference:' , dict[ 'ref' ] )
```

3 Now, display all keys within the dictionary
```
print( '\nKeys:' , dict.keys() )
```

4 Delete one pair from the dictionary and add a replacement pair then display the new key:value contents
```
del dict[ 'name' ]
dict[ 'user' ] = 'Tom'
print( '\nDictionary:' , dict )
```

5 Finally, search the dictionary for a specific key and display the result of the search
```
print( '\nIs There A name Key?:' ,'name' in dict )
```

6 Save the file in your scripts directory, then open a Command Prompt window there and run this program – to see the dictionary keys and values

```
Command Prompt                                    —    □    ×

C:\MyScripts>python dict.py
Dictionary: {'name': 'Bob', 'ref': 'Python', 'sys': 'Win'}

Reference: Python

Keys: dict_keys(['name', 'ref', 'sys'])

Dictionary: {'ref': 'Python', 'sys': 'Win', 'user': 'Tom'}

Is There A name Key?: False

C:\MyScripts>_
```

Beware

Notice that quotes must be preceded by a backslash escape character within a string – to prevent the string being prematurely terminated.

Indentation of code is very important in Python as it identifies code blocks to the interpreter – other programming languages use braces.

The **if: elif: else:** sequence is the Python equivalent of the **switch** or **case** statements found in other languages.

Branching with if

The Python **if** keyword performs the basic conditional test that evaluates a given expression for a Boolean value of **True** or **False**. This allows a program to proceed in different directions according to the result of the test, and is known as "conditional branching".

The tested expression must be followed by a : colon, then statements to be executed when the test succeeds should follow below on separate lines, and each line must be indented from the **if** test line. The size of the indentation is not important, but it must be the same for each line. So the syntax looks like this:

if *test-expression* :
>   *statements-to-execute-when-test-expression-is-True*
>   *statements-to-execute-when-test-expression-is-True*

Optionally, an **if** test can offer alternative statements to execute when the test fails by appending an **else** keyword after the statements to be executed when the test succeeds. The **else** keyword must be followed by a : colon and aligned with the **if** keyword, but its statements must be indented in a likewise manner, so its syntax looks like this:

if *test-expression* :
>   *statements-to-execute-when-test-expression-is-True*
>   *statements-to-execute-when-test-expression-is-True*

else :
>   *statements-to-execute-when-test-expression-is-False*
>   *statements-to-execute-when-test-expression-is-False*

An **if** test block can be followed by an alternative test using the **elif** keyword ("else if") that offers statements to be executed when the alternative test succeeds. This too must be aligned with the **if** keyword, followed by a : colon, and its statements indented. A final **else** keyword can then be added to offer alternative statements to execute when the test fails. The syntax for the complete **if-elif-else** structure looks like this:

if *test-expression-1* :
>   *statements-to-execute-when-test-expression-1-is-True*
>   *statements-to-execute-when-test-expression-1-is-True*

elif *test-expression-2* :
>   *statements-to-execute-when-test-expression-2-is-True*
>   *statements-to-execute-when-test-expression-2-is-True*

else :
>   *statements-to-execute-when-test-expressions-are-False*
>   *statements-to-execute-when-test-expressions-are-False*

...cont'd

1 Start a new Python script by initializing a variable with user input of an integer value
```
num = int( input( 'Please Enter A Number: ' ) )
```

if.py

2 Next, test the variable and display an appropriate response
```
if num > 5 :
        print( 'Number Exceeds 5' )
elif num < 5 :
        print( 'Number is Less Than 5' )
else :
        print( 'Number Is 5' )
```

3 Now, test the variable again using two expressions and display a response only upon success
```
if num > 7 and num < 9 :
        print( 'Number is 8' )
if num == 1 or num == 3 :
        print( 'Number Is 1 or 3' )
```

The user input is read as a string value by default, so must be cast as an **int** data type with **int()** for arithmetical comparison.

4 Save the file in your scripts directory, then open a Command Prompt window there and run this program – to see conditional branching

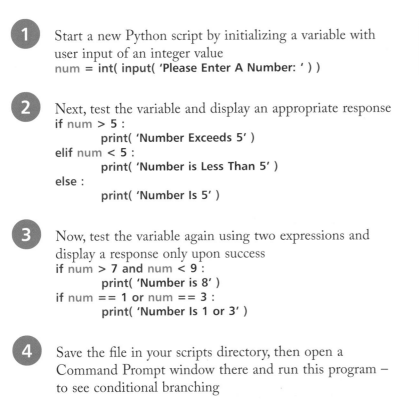

```
C:\MyScripts>python if.py
Please Enter A Number: 4
Number is Less Than 5

C:\MyScripts>python if.py
Please Enter A Number: 6
Number Exceeds 5

C:\MyScripts>python if.py
Please Enter A Number: 5
Number Is 5

C:\MyScripts>python if.py
Please Enter A Number: 3
Number is Less Than 5
Number Is 1 or 3

C:\MyScripts>_
```

The **and** keyword ensures the evaluation is **True** only when both tests succeed, whereas the **or** keyword ensures the evaluation is **True** when either test succeeds.

Looping while true

A loop is a piece of code in a program that automatically repeats. One complete execution of all statements within a loop is called an "iteration" or a "pass". The length of the loop is controlled by a conditional test made within the loop. While the tested expression is found to be **True**, the loop will continue – until the tested expression is found to be **False**, at which point the loop ends.

In Python programming, the **while** keyword creates a loop. It is followed by the test expression then a : colon character. Statements to be executed when the test succeeds should follow below on separate lines, and each line must be indented the same space from the **while** test line. This statement block must include a statement that will at some point change the result of the test expression evaluation – otherwise an infinite loop is created.

Indentation of code blocks must also be observed in Python's interactive mode – like this example that produces a Fibonacci sequence of numbers from a **while** loop:

Unlike other Python keywords, the keywords **True** and **False** begin with uppercase letters.

```
Python 3.7.0 Shell                                    —    □    ✕
File  Edit  Shell  Debug  Options  Window  Help
>>> a , b = 0 , 1
>>> while b < 100 :
        print( b )
        a , b = b , a + b


1
1
2
3
5
8
13
21
34
55
89
>>> |
                                                    Ln: 20  Col: 4
```

Hit Return to move to the next line and see the interpreter automatically indent the new line as it expects further statements. Hit Return again to execute the entered code.

Loops can be nested, one within another, to allow complete execution of all iterations of an inner nested loop on each iteration of the outer loop. A "counter" variable can be initialized with a starting value immediately before each loop definition, included in the test expression, and incremented on each iteration until the test fails – at which point the loop ends.

1 Start a new Python script by initializing a "counter" variable and define an outer loop using that variable in its test expression

```
i = 1
while i < 4 :
```

while.py

2 Next, add <u>indented</u> statements to display the counter's value and increment its value on each iteration of the loop

```
    print( '\nOuter Loop Iteration:' , i )
    i += 1
```

Hot tip

3 Now, (still indented) initialize a second "counter" variable and define an inner loop using this variable in its test expression

```
        j = 1
        while j < 4 :
```

The output printed from the inner loop is indented from that of the outer loop by the **\t** tab character.

4 Finally, add <u>further-indented</u> statements to display this counter's value and increment its value on each iteration

```
            print( '\tInner Loop Iteration:' , j  )
            j += 1
```

5 Save the file in your scripts directory, then open a Command Prompt window there and run this program – to see the output displayed on each loop iteration

```
C:\MyScripts>python while.py

Outer Loop Iteration: 1
        Inner Loop Iteration: 1
        Inner Loop Iteration: 2
        Inner Loop Iteration: 3

Outer Loop Iteration: 2
        Inner Loop Iteration: 1
        Inner Loop Iteration: 2
        Inner Loop Iteration: 3

Outer Loop Iteration: 3
        Inner Loop Iteration: 1
        Inner Loop Iteration: 2
        Inner Loop Iteration: 3

C:\MyScripts>
```

Hot tip

The **+=** assignment statement **i += 1** is simply a shorthand way to say **i = i+1** – you can also use ***= /= -=** shorthand to assign values to variables.

Looping over items

In Python programming, the **for** keyword loops over all items in any list specified to the **in** keyword. This statement must end with a : colon character, and statements to be executed on each iteration of the loop must be indented below, like this:

for *each-item* **in** *list-name* :
        statements-to-execute-on-each-iteration
        statements-to-execute-on-each-iteration

As a string is simply a list of characters, the **for in** statement can loop over each character. Similarly, a **for in** statement can loop over each element in a list, each item in a tuple, each member of a set, or each key in a dictionary.

A **for in** loop iterates over the items of any list or string in the order that they appear in the sequence, but you cannot directly specify the number of iterations to make, a halting condition, or the size of iteration step. You can, however, use the Python **range()** function to iterate over a sequence of numbers by specifying a numeric end value within its parameters. This will generate a sequence that starts at zero and continues up to, but not including, the specified end value. For example, **range(5)** generates 0,1,2,3,4.

Optionally, you can specify both a start and end value within the parentheses of the **range()** function, separated by a comma. For example, **range(1,5)** generates 1,2,3,4. Also, you can specify a start value, end value, and a step value to the **range()** function as a comma-separated list within its parentheses. For example, **range(1,14,4)** generates 1,5,9,13.

You can specify the list's name within the parentheses of Python's **enumerate()** function to display each element's index number and its associated value.

When looping through multiple lists simultaneously, the element values of the same index number in each list can be displayed together by specifying the list names as a comma-separated list within the parentheses of Python's **zip()** function.

When looping through a dictionary you can display each key and its associated value using the dictionary **items()** method and specifying two comma-separated variable names to the **for** keyword – one for the key name and the other for its value.

The **range()** function can generate a sequence that decreases, counting down, as well as those that count upward.

The **for** loop in Python is unlike that in other languages such as C, as it does not allow step size and end to be specified.

...cont'd

for.py

1 Start a new Python script by initializing a list, a tuple, and a dictionary

```
chars = [ 'A' , 'B', 'C' ]
fruit = ( 'Apple' , 'Banana' , 'Cherry' )
dict = { 'name' : 'Mike' , 'ref' : 'Python' , 'sys' : 'Win' }
```

2 Next, add statements to display all list element values

```
print( '\nElements:\t' , end = ' ' )
for item in chars :
        print( item , end = ' ' )
```

3 Now, add statements to display all list element values and their relative index number

```
print( '\nEnumerated:\t' , end = ' ' )
for item in enumerate( chars ) :
        print( item , end = ' ' )
```

4 Then, add statements to display all list and tuple elements

```
print( '\nZipped:\t' , end = ' ' )
for item in zip( chars , fruit ) :
        print( item , end = ' ' )
```

5 Finally, add statements to display all dictionary key names and associated element values

```
print( '\nPaired:' )
for key , value in dict.items() :
        print( key , '=' , value )
```

6 Save the file in your scripts directory, then open a Command Prompt window there and run this program – to see the items displayed by the loop iterations

```
C:\MyScripts>python for.py

Elements:         A B C
Enumerated:       (0, 'A') (1, 'B') (2, 'C')
Zipped:  ('A', 'Apple') ('B', 'Banana') ('C', 'Cherry')
Paired:
name = Mike
ref = Python
sys = Win

C:\MyScripts>
```

Hot tip

In Python programming anything that contains multiple items that can be looped over is described as "iterable".

Breaking out of loops

The Python **break** keyword can be used to prematurely terminate a loop when a specified condition is met. The **break** statement is situated inside the loop statement block and is preceded by a test expression. When the test returns **True**, the loop ends immediately and the program proceeds on to the next task. For example, in a nested inner loop it proceeds to the next iteration of the outer loop.

nest.py

 1 Start a new Python script with a statement creating a loop that iterates three times
for i **in range(1, 4) :**

 2 Next, add an indented statement creating a "nested" inner loop that also iterates three times
for j **in range(1, 4) :**

3 Now, add a further-indented statement in the inner loop to display the counter numbers (of both the outer loop and the inner loop) on each iteration of the inner loop
print('Running i=' , i **, ' j=' ,** j **)**

4 Save the file in your scripts directory, then open a Command Prompt window there and run this program – to see the counter values on each loop iteration

```
C:\MyScripts>python nest.py
Running i = 1   j = 1
Running i = 1   j = 2
Running i = 1   j = 3
Running i = 2   j = 1
Running i = 2   j = 2
Running i = 2   j = 3
Running i = 3   j = 1
Running i = 3   j = 2
Running i = 3   j = 3

C:\MyScripts>
```

Hot tip

Compare these nested **for** loops with the nested **while** loops example on page 55.

5 Now, insert this **break** statement at the very beginning of the inner loop block, to break out of the inner loop – then save the file and run the program once more

break.py

```
if i == 2 and j == 1 :
    print( 'Breaks inner loop at i=2 j=1' )
    break
```

```
Command Prompt                              —  □  ×

C:\MyScripts>python break.py
Running i = 1  j = 1
Running i = 1  j = 2
Running i = 1  j = 3
Breaks inner loop at i=2 j=1
Running i = 3  j = 1
Running i = 3  j = 2
Running i = 3  j = 3

C:\MyScripts>
```

Here, the **break** statement halts all three iterations of the inner loop when the outer loop tries to run it the second time.

The Python **continue** keyword can be used to skip a single iteration of a loop when a specified condition is met. The **continue** statement is situated inside the loop statement block and is preceded by a test expression. When the test returns **True**, that one iteration ends and the program proceeds to the next iteration.

6 Insert this continue statement at the beginning of the inner loop block, to skip the first iteration of the inner loop – then save the file and run the program again

continue.py

```
if i == 1 and j == 1 :
    print( 'Continues inner loop at i=1 j=1' )
    continue
```

```
Command Prompt                              —  □  ×

C:\MyScripts>python continue.py
Continues inner loop at i=1 j=1
Running i = 1  j = 2
Running i = 1  j = 3
Breaks inner loop at i=2 j=1
Running i = 3  j = 1
Running i = 3  j = 2
Running i = 3  j = 3

C:\MyScripts>
```

Here, the **continue** statement just skips the first iteration of the inner loop when the outer loop tries to run it for the first time.

Summary

- In Python, multiple assignments can be used to initialize several variables in a single statement.

- A Python list is a variable that can store multiple items of data in sequentially-numbered elements that start at zero.

- Data stored in a list element can be referenced using the list name followed by an index number in [ ] square brackets.

- The **len()** function returns the length of a specified list.

- A Python tuple is an immutable list whose values can be assigned to individual variables by "sequence unpacking".

- Data stored in a tuple element can be referenced using the tuple name followed by an index number in [ ] square brackets.

- A Python set is an unordered collection of unique elements whose values can be compared and manipulated by its methods.

- Data stored in a set cannot be referenced by index number.

- A Python dictionary is a list of key:value pairs of data in which each key must be unique.

- Data stored in a dictionary element can be referenced using the dictionary name followed by its key in [ ] square brackets.

- The Python **if** keyword performs a conditional test on an expression for a Boolean value of **True** or **False**.

- Conditional branching provides alternatives to an **if** test with the **else** and **elif** keywords.

- A **while** loop repeats until a test expression returns **False**.

- A **for in** loop iterates over each item in a specified list or string.

- The **range()** function generates a numerical sequence that can be used to specify the length of a **for in** loop.

- The **break** and **continue** keywords interrupt loop iterations.

4 Defining functions

This chapter demonstrates how to create functions that can be called to execute statements when the program requires them.

Function statements must be indented from the definition line by the same amount so the Python interpreter can recognize the block.

Understanding scope

Previous examples in this book have used built-in functions of the Python programming language, such as the **print()** function. However, most Python programs contain a number of custom functions that can be called as required when the program runs.

A custom function is created using the **def** (definition) keyword followed by a name of your choice and **( )** parentheses. The programmer can choose any name for a function except the Python keywords listed on the inside front cover of this book, and the name of an existing built-in function. This line must end with a : colon character, then the statements to be executed whenever the function gets called must appear on lines below and be indented. Syntax of a function definition, therefore, looks like this:

def *function-name* **( ) :**
      statements-to-be-executed
      statements-to-be-executed

Once the function statements have been executed, program flow resumes at the point directly following the function call. This modularity is very useful in Python programming to isolate set routines so they can be called upon repeatedly.

To create custom functions it is necessary to understand the accessibility ("scope") of variables in a program:

- Variables created outside functions can be referenced by statements inside functions – they have "global" scope.

- Variables created inside functions cannot be referenced from outside the function in which they have been created – these have "local" scope.

The limited accessibility of local variables means that variables of the same name can appear in different functions without conflict.

If you want to coerce a local variable to make it accessible elsewhere, it must first be declared with the Python **global** keyword followed by its name only. It may subsequently be assigned a value that can be referenced from anywhere in the program. Where a global variable and a local variable have the same name, the function will use the local version.

Avoid using global variables in order to prevent accidental conflict – use only local variables where possible.

...cont'd

1 Start a new Python script by initializing a global variable
```
global_var = 1
```

scope.py

2 Next, create a function named "my_vars" to display the value contained within the global variable
```
def my_vars() :
        print( 'Global Variable:' , global_var )
```

3 Now, add indented statements to the function block to initialize a local variable and display the value it contains
```
        local_var = 2
        print( 'Local variable:' , local_var )
```

4 Then, add indented statements to the function block to create a coerced global variable and assign an initial value
```
        global inner_var
        inner_var = 3
```

5 Add a statement after the function to call upon that function to execute the statements it contains
```
my_vars()
```

6 Finally, add a statement to display the value contained in the coerced global variable
```
print( 'Coerced Global:' , inner_var )
```

7 Save the file in your scripts directory, then open a Command Prompt window there and run this program – to see the custom function display the variable values

```
Command Prompt                                    —  □  ×

C:\MyScripts>python scope.py
Global Variable: 1
Local Variable: 2
Coerced Global: 3

C:\MyScripts>
```

Hot tip

Variables that are not global but appear in some outer scope can be addressed using the **nonlocal** keyword.

Supplying arguments

When defining a custom function in Python programming you may, optionally, specify an "argument" name between the function's parentheses. A value can then be passed to that argument by specifying the value in the parentheses of the call to the function. The function can now use that passed in value during its execution by referencing it via the argument name. For example, defining a function to accept an argument to print out, like this:

```
def echo( user ) :
        print( 'User:' , user )
```

A call to this function must specify a value to be passed to the argument within its parentheses so it can be printed out:

```
echo( 'Mike' )
```

Multiple arguments (a.k.a. "parameters") can be specified in the function definition by including a comma-separated list of argument names within the function parentheses:

```
def echo( user , lang ,  sys ) :
        print( User:' , user , 'Language:' , lang , 'Platform:' , sys )
```

When calling a function whose definition specifies arguments, the call must include the same number of data values as arguments. For example, to call this example with multiple arguments:

```
echo( 'Mike' , 'Python' , 'Windows' )
```

The passed values must appear in the same order as the arguments list unless the caller also specifies the argument names, like this:

```
echo( lang = 'Python' , user = 'Mike' , sys = 'Windows' )
```

Optionally, a default value may be specified in the argument list when defining a function. This will be overridden when the caller specifies a value for that argument, but will be used by the function when no value gets passed by the caller:

```
def echo( user , lang ,  sys = 'Linux' ) :
        print( User:' , user , 'Language:' , lang , 'Platform:' , sys )
```

This means you may call the function passing fewer values than the number of arguments specified in the function definition, to use the default argument value, or pass the same number of values as specified arguments to override the default value.

Argument-naming follows the same conventions as variables and functions.

Name arguments the same as variables passed to them to make the data movement obvious.

1 Start a new Python script by defining a function to accept three arguments that will print out their passed in values

```python
def echo( user , lang , sys ) :
        print( 'User:', user, 'Language:', lang, 'Platform:', sys )
```

args.py

2 Next, call the function passing string values to the function arguments in the order they appear

```python
echo( 'Mike' , 'Python' , 'Windows' )
```

3 Now, call the function passing string values to the function arguments by specifying the argument names

```python
echo( lang = 'Python' , sys = 'Mac OS' , user = 'Anne' )
```

4 Then, define another function to accept two arguments with default values that will print out argument values

```python
def mirror(  user = 'Carole' , lang = 'Python' ) :
        print( '\nUser:' , user , 'Language:' , lang )
```

5 Finally, add statements to call the second function both using and overriding default values

```python
mirror()
mirror( lang = 'Java' )
mirror( user = 'Tony' )
mirror( 'Susan' , 'C++' )
```

6 Save the file in your scripts directory, then open a Command Prompt window there and run this program – to see the function display the argument values

```
Command Prompt                                    —    □    ×

C:\MyScripts>python args.py
User: Mike Language: Python Platform: Windows
User: Anne Language: Python Platform: Mac OS

User: Carole Language: Python

User: Carole Language: Java

User: Tony Language: Python

User: Susan Language: C++

C:\MyScripts>_
```

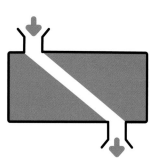

Returning values

Like Python's built-in **str()** function, which returns a string representation of the value specified as its argument by the caller, custom functions can also return a value to their caller by using the Python **return** keyword to specify a value to be returned. For example, to return to the caller the total of adding two specified argument values, like this:

```
def sum( a , b ) :
        return a + b
```

The returned result may be assigned to a variable by the caller for subsequent use by the program, like this:

```
total = sum( 8 , 4 )
print( 'Eight Plus Four Is:' , total )
```

Or the returned result may be used directly "in-line", like this:

```
print( 'Eight Plus Four Is:' , sum( 8 , 4 ) )
```

Typically, a **return** statement will appear at the very end of a function block to return the final result of executing all statements contained in that function.

A **return** statement may, however, appear earlier in the function block to halt execution of all subsequent statements in that block. This immediately resumes execution of the program at the caller. Optionally, the **return** statement may specify a value to be returned to the caller or the value may be omitted. Where no value is specified, a default value of **None** is assumed. Typically, this is used to halt execution of the function statements after a conditional test is found to be **False**. For example, where a passed argument value is below a specified number:

```
def sum( a , b ) :
        if a < 5 :
                return
        return a + b
```

In this case, the function will return the default value **None** when the first passed argument value is below five and the final statement will not be executed.

Where the function is to perform arithmetic, user input can be validated for integer values with the built-in **isdigit()** function.

Don't forget

You can specify a default value for an argument in the function definition.

1 Start a new Python script by initializing a variable with user input of an integer value for manipulation

```
num = input( 'Enter An Integer:' )
```

return.py

2 Next, add a function definition that accepts a single argument value to be passed from the caller

```
def square( num ) :
```

3 Now, insert into the function block an indented statement to validate the passed value as an integer or halt further execution of the function's statements

```
        if not num.isdigit() :
                return 'Invalid Entry'
```

4 Then, add indented statements to cast the passed value as an **int** data type then return the sum of squaring that value to the caller

```
        num = int( num )
        return num * num
```

5 Finally, add a statement to output a string and the returned value from the function call

```
print( num , 'Squared Is:' , square( num ) )
```

6 Save the file in your scripts directory, then open a Command Prompt window there and run this program – to see the function display the returned values

```
C:\MyScripts>python return.py
Enter An Integer:8
8 Squared Is: 64

C:\MyScripts>python return.py
Enter An Integer:8.0
8.0 Squared Is: Invalid Entry

C:\MyScripts>python return.py
Enter An Integer:Eight
Eight Squared Is: Invalid Entry

C:\MyScripts>
```

Beware

Remember that user input is read as a **str** data type – so must be cast into an **int** or **float** data type for arithmetic.

Using callbacks

In Python, a named function is created using the **def** keyword to specify a function name, which can be used to call that function at any time in the program to execute the statements it contains. Optionally, the named function can return a value to the caller.

Python also allows an anonymous un-named function to be created using the **lambda** keyword. An anonymous function may only contain a single expression that must always return a value.

Unlike the usual creation of a function with the **def** keyword, the creation of a function with the **lambda** keyword returns a "function object". This can be assigned to a variable, which can then be used to reference ("call back") the function at any time in the program to execute the expression it contains.

The **lambda** keyword, therefore, offers the programmer an alternative syntax for the creation of a function. For example:

def square(x) :
    return x ** 2

can alternatively be written more succinctly as...

square = lambda x : x ** 2

In either case, the call **square(5)** returns the result 25 by passing in an integer argument to the function. Note that the **lambda** keyword is followed by an argument without parentheses, and the specified expression does not require the **return** keyword as all functions created with **lambda** must implicitly return a value.

While the **lambda** keyword offers an alternative way to create a function it is mostly used to embed a function within the code. For instance, callbacks are frequently coded as inline **lambda** expressions embedded directly in a caller's arguments list – instead of being defined with the **def** keyword elsewhere in the program and referenced by name. For example:

def function_1 : *statements-to-be-executed*
def function_2 : *statements-to-be-executed*
callbacks = [function_1 , function_2]

can alternatively be written more succinctly as...

callbacks = [lambda : *expression* , lambda : *expression*]

Hot tip

In-line **lambda** callbacks are often used to define the behavior of buttons in a GUI program.

68

1 Start a new Python script by defining three functions to return a passed argument raised to various powers
```
def function_1( x ) : return x ** 2
def function_2( x ) : return x ** 3
def function_3( x ) : return x ** 4
```

PY

lambda.py

2 Next, add a statement to create a list of callbacks to each of the functions by referencing their names
```
callbacks = [ function_1 , function_2 , function_3 ]
```

3 Now, display a heading and the result of passing a value to each of the named functions
```
print( '\nNamed Functions:' )
for function in callbacks : print( 'Result:' , function( 3 ) )
```

Hot tip

Function definitions that contain just one statement can be written on just one line – as seen here.

4 Then, add a statement to create a list of callbacks to in-line anonymous functions that return a passed argument raised to various powers
```
callbacks = \
[ lambda x : x ** 2 , lambda x : x ** 3 , lambda x : x ** 4 ]
```

Hot tip

5 Finally, display a heading and the result of passing a value to each of the anonymous functions
```
print( '\nAnonymous Functions:' )
for function in callbacks : print( 'Result:' , function( 3 ) )
```

The \ backslash character can be used to allow code to continue on the next line – as seen here.

6 Save the file in your scripts directory, then open a Command Prompt window there and run this program – to see returns from regular and anonymous functions

```
Command Prompt                          —    □    ×

C:\MyScripts>python lambda.py

Named Functions:
Result: 9
Result: 27
Result: 81

Anonymous Functions:
Result: 9
Result: 27
Result: 81

C:\MyScripts>_
```

Adding placeholders

The Python **pass** keyword is useful when writing program code as a temporary placeholder that can be inserted into the code at places where further code needs to be added later. The **pass** keyword is inserted where a statement is required syntactically, but it merely performs a "null" operation – when it is executed nothing happens and no code needs to be executed. This allows an incomplete program to be executed for testing by simulating correct syntax so the interpreter does not report errors.

incomplete.py

1. Start a new Python script by initializing a variable with a Boolean value, then add an incomplete conditional test

```
bool = True
if bool :
        print( 'Python In Easy Steps' )
else :
        # Statements to be inserted here.
```

2. Save the file in your scripts directory, then open a Command Prompt window there and run this program – to see the interpreter report an error

```
Command Prompt

C:\MyScripts>python incomplete.py
  File "incomplete.py", line 7

                                        ^
SyntaxError: unexpected EOF while parsing

C:\MyScripts>_
```

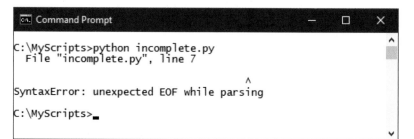

pass.py

3. Replace the comment with the **pass** keyword then save the file and run the program again – to see the program execute as the interpreter does not now find an error

```
Command Prompt

C:\MyScripts>python pass.py
Python In Easy Steps

C:\MyScripts>_
```

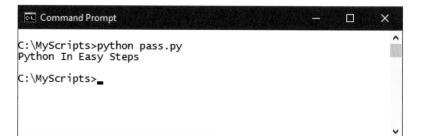

...cont'd

In loop structures it is important not to confuse the **pass** keyword, which allows the interpreter to process all subsequent statements on that iteration, with the **continue** keyword, which skips subsequent statements on that iteration of the loop only.

① Start a new Python script by initializing a variable with a string value
```
title = '\nPython In Easy Steps\n'
```

skip.py

② Next, add a loop to print each character of the string
```
for char in title : print( char , end = ' ' )
```

③ Now, add a loop that prints each string character but replaces any 'y' character then skips to the next iteration
```
for char in title :
        if char == 'y' :
                print( '*' , end = ' ' )
                continue
        print( char , end = ' ' )
```

④ Finally, add a loop that prints each string character but inserts an asterisk before each 'y' character
```
for char in title :
        if char == 'y' :
                print( '*' , end = ' ' )
                pass
        print( char , end = ' ' )
```

⑤ Save the file in your scripts directory, then open a Command Prompt window there and run this program – to see a different output from each loop

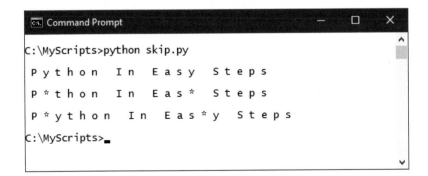

```
C:\MyScripts>python skip.py
P y t h o n    I n    E a s y    S t e p s
P * t h o n    I n    E a s *    S t e p s
P * y t h o n    I n    E a s * y    S t e p s
C:\MyScripts>
```

In a loop, the **continue** keyword continues on the next iteration, whereas the **pass** keyword passes on to the next statement of the same iteration.

Producing generators

When a Python function is called, it executes the statements it contains and may return any value specified to the **return** keyword. After the function ends, control returns to the caller and the state of the function is not retained. When the function is next called, it will process its statements from start to finish once more.

A Python generator, on the other hand, is a special function that returns a "generator object" to the caller rather than a data value. This, effectively, retains the state of the function when it was last called, so it will continue from that point when next called.

Generator functions are produced by definition just like regular functions, but contain a "yield" statement. This begins with the Python **yield** keyword and specifies the generator object to be returned to the caller. When the yield statement gets executed, the state of the generator object is frozen, and the current value in its "expression list" is retained. The generator object returned by the yield statement can be conveniently assigned to a variable. Python's built-in **next()** function can then specify that variable name within its parentheses to continue execution of the function from the point at which it was frozen – exactly as if the yield statement were just another external call.

Repeatedly calling the generator object with the **next()** function continues execution of the function until it raises an exception. This can be avoided by enclosing the yield statement within an infinite loop so it will return successive values on each iteration. For example, to yield an incremented value on each call:

```
def incrementer() :
        i = 1
        while True :
                yield i
                i += 1

inc = incrementer()

print( next( inc ) )
print( next( inc ) )
print( next( inc ) )
```

These calls display the integer value 1, then 2, then 3.

Perhaps more usefully, the generator object can be referenced from a loop to successively iterate through values.

Changing the conditional test in this loop to read **while i < 3** will cause a StopIteration error when called for the third time.

...cont'd

1 Start a new Python script by defining a function that begins by initializing two variables with an integer of one

```python
def fibonacci_generator() :
    a = b = 1
```

yield.py

2 Next, in the function body insert an indented infinite loop to yield the addition of two previous values

```python
while True :
    yield a
    a , b = b , a + b
```

3 Now, assign the returned generator object to a variable

```python
fib = fibonacci_generator()
```

Here, the variables are initialized with a common value in a single statement.

4 Finally, add a loop to successively call the generator function and display its value on each iteration

```python
for i in fib :
    if i > 100 :
        break
    else :
        print( 'Generated:' , i )
```

5 Save the file in your scripts directory, then open a Command Prompt window there and run this program – to see the loop display increasing generated values

```
Command Prompt                                    □   ×

C:\MyScripts>python yield.py
Generated: 1
Generated: 1
Generated: 2
Generated: 3
Generated: 5
Generated: 8
Generated: 13
Generated: 21
Generated: 34
Generated: 55
Generated: 89

C:\MyScripts>_
```

You can use the in-built **type()** function to confirm the object type – here, **type(fib)** is confirmed as a generator class object.

Handling exceptions

Sections of a Python script in which it is possible to anticipate errors, such as those handling user input, can be enclosed in a **try except** block to handle "exception errors". The statements to be executed are grouped in a **try** : block, and exceptions are passed to the ensuing **except** : block for handling. Optionally, this may be followed by a **finally** : block containing statements to be executed after exceptions have been handled.

Python recognizes many built-in exceptions such as the **NameError**, which occurs when a variable name is not found, the **IndexError**, which occurs when trying to address a non-existent list index, and the **ValueError**, which occurs when a built-in operation or function receives an argument that has an inappropriate value.

Each exception returns a descriptive message that can, usefully, be assigned to a variable with the **as** keyword. This can then be used to display the nature of the exception when it occurs.

Hot tip

Discover more built-in exceptions online at **http://docs.python.org/3/ library/exceptions.html**

try.py

1 Start a new Python script by initializing a variable with a string value
title = 'Python In Easy Steps'

2 Next, add a try statement block that attempts to display the variable value – but specifies the name incorrectly
try :
   print(titel)

3 Now, add an except statement block to display an error message when a NameError occurs
except NameError as msg :
   print(msg)

4 Save the file in your scripts directory, then open a Command Prompt window there and run this program – to see how the error gets handled

```
Command Prompt                            —    □    ×

C:\MyScripts>python try.py
name 'titel' is not defined

C:\MyScripts>_
```

Multiple exceptions can be handled by specifying their type as a comma-separated list in parentheses within the except block:

```
except ( NameError , IndexError ) as msg :
        print( msg )
```

You can also compel the interpreter to report an exception by using the **raise** keyword to specify the type of exception to be recognized and a custom descriptive message in parentheses.

 1 Start a new Python script by initializing a variable with an integer value
```
day = 32
```

raise.py

 2 Next, add a try statement block that tests the variable value then specifies an exception and custom message
```
try :
        if day > 31 :
                raise ValueError( 'Invalid Day Number' )
        # More statements to execute get added here.
```

 3 Now, add an except statement block to display an error message when a ValueError occurs
```
except ValueError as msg :
        print( 'The Program found An' , msg )
```

 4 Then, add a finally statement block to display a message after the exception has been handled successfully
```
finally :
        print( 'But Today Is Beautiful Anyway.' )
```

 5 Save the file in your scripts directory, then open a Command Prompt window there and run this program – to see the raised error get handled

Statements in the try block are all executed unless or until an exception occurs.

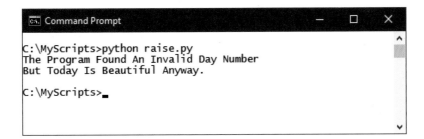

```
C:\MyScripts>python raise.py
The Program Found An Invalid Day Number
But Today Is Beautiful Anyway.

C:\MyScripts>
```

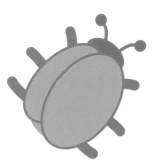

Debugging assertions

When tracking down (debugging) errors in your code it is often useful to "comment-out" one or more lines of code by prefixing each line with the **#** hash character – as used for your comments. The Python interpreter will then omit execution of those lines so helps to localize where a problem lies. For example, where you suspect a variable assignment problem it can be excluded, like this:

 # elem = elem / 2

If the program now runs without errors, the commented-out assignment can be assumed to be problematic.

Another useful debugging technique employs the Python **assert** keyword to add error-checking code to your script. This examines a specified test expression for a Boolean **True** or **False** result, and reports an "AssertionError" when the test fails. Optionally, an **assert** statement can include a descriptive message to supply when reporting an AssertionError, and has this syntax:

assert *test-expression , descriptive-message*

When the test expression fails, the interpreter reports the AssertionError and halts execution of the script, but when the test succeeds, the **assert** statement does nothing, and execution of the script continues.

Employing **assert** statements is an effective way to document your script, as their descriptive messages provide commentary and their tests alert you when your code is erroneous.

Assert versus Exception
At first glance, an AssertionError can appear confusingly similar to an Exception, but it is important to recognize their distinctions:

- **Exceptions** provide a way to handle errors that may legitimately occur at runtime.

- **AssertionErrors** provide a way to alert the programmer to mistakes during development.

Typically, **assert** statements will be removed from release versions of a program after debugging is complete, whereas **except** statements will remain to handle runtime errors.

Hot tip

You can have the interpreter ignore all assert statements using a **-O** switch in the run command – for example, **python -O assert.py**

...cont'd

1   Start a new Python script by initializing a list with several string values
```
chars = [ 'Alpha' , 'Beta' , 'Gamma' , 'Delta' , 'Epsilon' ]
```

assert.py

2   Next, define a function to accept a single argument
```
def display( elem ) :
```

3   Now, add indented statements in the function body to ensure the passed argument value is an integer, then display a list element of that index number
```
        assert type( elem ) is int , 'Argument Must Be Integer!'
        print( 'List Element' , elem , '=' , chars[ elem ] )
```

4   Then, initialize a variable with an integer value and call the function, passing this variable value as its argument
```
elem = 4
display( elem )
```

5   Finally, change the variable value, then call the function once more, passing the new variable value as its argument
```
elem = elem / 2
display( elem )
```

6   Save the file in your scripts directory, then open a Command Prompt window there and run this program – to see an AssertionError reported

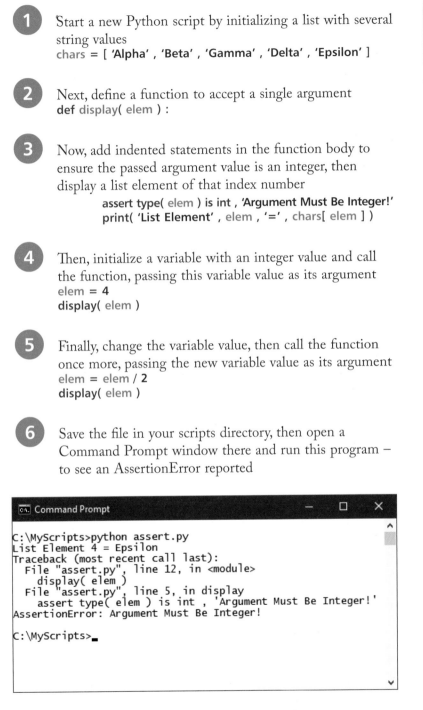

```
C:\MyScripts>python assert.py
List Element 4 = Epsilon
Traceback (most recent call last):
  File "assert.py", line 12, in <module>
    display( elem )
  File "assert.py", line 5, in display
    assert type( elem ) is int , 'Argument Must Be Integer!'
AssertionError: Argument Must Be Integer!

C:\MyScripts>
```

This **AssertionError** occurs because the division operation returns a float value, not an integer value.

Summary

- Functions are defined using the **def** keyword, and contain indented statements to execute when the function gets called.

- Variables with global scope can be referenced from anywhere, but variables with local scope can only be referenced from within the function in which they are declared.

- Arguments are declared as a comma-separated list within the parentheses of a function definition.

- Function calls must supply data for each function argument unless a default value is specified in their declaration.

- Optionally, a function can include a **return** statement to return a value to the caller.

- An anonymous function containing a single expression is created with the **lambda** keyword, and returns a function object.

- Callbacks are frequently coded as inline **lambda** expressions embedded directly in a caller's argument list.

- Placeholders can be created by inserting the **pass** keyword where a statement is required syntactically.

- A generator function is created when a statement using the **yield** keyword appears in its function block.

- Generator functions retain the state of the function when last called, and return a generator object to the caller.

- The built-in **next()** function can be used to continue execution of a generator function from the point where it was frozen.

- Anticipated runtime exception errors can be handled by enclosing statements in a **try except** block.

- Optionally, a **finally** statement can be used to specify statements to be executed after exceptions have been handled.

- Error-checking code can be added to scripts using the **assert** keyword to report development errors.

5 Importing modules

This chapter demonstrates how to use Python modules in your programs.

Storing functions

Python function definitions can, usefully, be stored in one or more separate files for easier maintenance and to allow them to be used in several programs without copying the definitions into each one. Each file storing function definitions is called a "module" and the module name is the file name without the ".py" extension.

Functions stored in the module are made available to a program using the Python **import** keyword followed by the module name. Although not essential, it is customary to put any **import** statements at the beginning of the program.

Imported functions can be called using their name dot-suffixed after the module name. For example, a "steps" function from an imported module named "ineasy" can be called with **ineasy.steps()**.

Where functions stored in a module include arguments, it is often useful to assign a default value to the argument in the definition. This makes the function more versatile, as it becomes optional for the call to specify an argument value.

cat.py

1. Start a new Python module by defining a function that supplies a default string value to its argument for display
   def purr(pet = 'A Cat') :
           print(pet , 'Says MEOW!')

2. Next, add two more function definitions that also supply default string values to their arguments for display
   def lick(pet = 'A Cat') :
           print(pet , 'Drinks Milk')

   def nap(pet = 'A Cat') :
           print(pet , 'Sleeps By The Fire')

3. Now, save the file as "cat.py" so the module is named "cat"

kitty.py

4. Start a new Python script with a statement to make the "cat" module functions available
   import cat

5. Next, call each function without supplying an argument
   cat.purr()
   cat.lick()
   cat.nap()

...cont'd

6 Now, call each function again and pass an argument to each, then save the file

```
cat.purr( 'Kitty' )
cat.lick( 'Kitty' )
cat.nap( 'Kitty' )
```

7 Start another Python script by making the "cat" module functions available once more

```
import cat
```

8 Then, request the user enters a name to overwrite the default argument value

```
pet = input( 'Enter A Pet Name: ' )
```

tiger.py

9 Finally, call each function, passing the user-defined value as the argument

```
cat.purr( pet )
cat.lick( pet )
cat.nap( pet )
```

10 Save the file in your scripts directory, then open a Command Prompt window there and run these programs – to see output from the imported module

```
C:\MyScripts>python kitty.py
A Cat Says MEOW!
A Cat Drinks Milk
A Cat Sleeps By The Fire
Kitty Says MEOW!
Kitty Drinks Milk
Kitty Sleeps By The Fire

C:\MyScripts>python tiger.py
Enter A Pet Name: Tiger
Tiger Says MEOW!
Tiger Drinks Milk
Tiger Sleeps By The Fire

C:\MyScripts>
```

You can create an alias when importing a module using **import as** keywords. For example, **import cat as tom** allows you to use **tom** as the function prefix in calls.

Owning function names

Internally, each Python module and program has its own "symbol table" that is used by all functions defined in that context only. This avoids possible conflicts with functions of the same name in another module if both modules were imported into one program.

When you import a module with an **import** statement, that module's symbol table does not get added to the program's symbol table – only the module's name gets added. That is why you need to call the module's functions using their module name prefix. Importing a "steps" function from a module named "ineasy" and another "steps" function from a module named "dance" means they can be called without conflict as **ineasy.steps()** and **dance.steps()**.

Generally, it is preferable to avoid conflicts by importing the module name and calling its functions with the module name prefix, but you can import individual function names instead with a **from import** statement. The module name is specified after the **from** keyword, and functions to import are specified as a comma-separated list after the **import** keyword. Alternatively, the * wildcard character can be specified after **import** to import all function names into the program's own symbol table. This means the functions can be called without a module name prefix.

Don't forget

Where you import individual function names, the module name does not get imported – so it cannot be used as a prefix.

82

dog.py

1. Start a new Python module by defining a function that supplies a default string value to its argument
```python
def bark( pet = 'A Dog' ) :
        print( pet , 'Says WOOF!' )
```

2. Next, add two more function definitions that also supply default string values to their arguments
```python
def lick( pet = 'A Dog' ) :
        print( pet , 'Drinks water' )

def nap( pet = 'A Dog' ) :
        print( pet , ' Sleeps In The Sun' )
```

3. Save the file as "dog.py" so the module is named "dog"

4. Start a new Python script with a statement to make individual "dog" module functions available
```python
from dog import bark , lick , nap
```

pooch.py

5 Next, call each function without supplying an argument
```
bark()
lick()
nap()
```

6 Now, call each function again and pass an argument value
to each then save the file
```
bark( 'Pooch' )
lick( 'Pooch' )
nap( 'Pooch' )
```

7 Start another Python script by making all "dog" module
functions available
```
from dog import *
```

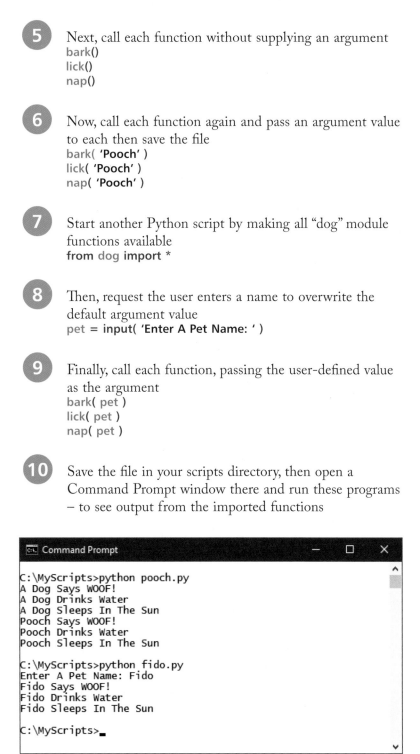

fido.py

8 Then, request the user enters a name to overwrite the
default argument value
```
pet = input( 'Enter A Pet Name: ' )
```

9 Finally, call each function, passing the user-defined value
as the argument
```
bark( pet )
lick( pet )
nap( pet )
```

10 Save the file in your scripts directory, then open a
Command Prompt window there and run these programs
– to see output from the imported functions

```
Command Prompt                              —    □    ×

C:\MyScripts>python pooch.py
A Dog Says WOOF!
A Dog Drinks Water
A Dog Sleeps In The Sun
Pooch Says WOOF!
Pooch Drinks Water
Pooch Sleeps In The Sun

C:\MyScripts>python fido.py
Enter A Pet Name: Fido
Fido Says WOOF!
Fido Drinks Water
Fido Sleeps In The Sun

C:\MyScripts>_
```

For larger programs you
can import modules into
other modules to build a
module hierarchy.

Interrogating the system

Python includes "sys" and "keyword" modules that are useful for interrogating the Python system itself. The keyword module contains a list of all Python keywords in its **kwlist** attribute, and provides an **iskeyword()** method if you want to test a word.

You can explore the many features of the "sys" module, and indeed any feature of Python, using the Interactive Mode help system. Just type **help()** at the **>>>** prompt to start the help system, then type **sys** at the **help>** prompt that appears.

Perhaps most usefully, the "sys" module has attributes that contain the Python version number, interpreter location on your system, and a list of all directories where the interpreter seeks module files – so if you save module files in any of these directories you can be sure the interpreter will find them.

system.py

 Start a new Python script by importing the "sys" and "keyword" modules to make their features available
import sys , keyword

 Next, add a statement to display the Python version
print('Python Version:' , sys.version)

 Now, add a statement to display the actual location on your system of the Python interpreter
print('Python Interpreter Location:' , sys.executable)

 Then, add statements to display a list of all directories where the Python interpreter looks for module files
print('Python Module Search Path: ')
for dir in sys.path :
  print(dir)

5 Finally, add statements to display a list of all the Python keywords
print('Python Keywords: ')
for word in keyword.kwlist :
  print(word)

6 Save the file in your scripts directory, then open a Command Prompt window there and run this program – to see details of the Python version on your system

```
Command Prompt                                    —    □    ✕

C:\MyScripts>python system.py
Python Version: 3.7.0
Python Interpreter Location: C:\Python37\python.exe
Python Module Search Path:
C:\MyScripts
C:\Python37\python37.zip
C:\Python37\DLLs
C:\Python37\lib
C:\Python37
C:\Python37\lib\site-packages
Python Keywords:
False
None
True
and
as
assert
async
await
break
class
continue
def
del
elif
else
except
finally
for
from
global
if
import
in
is
lambda
nonlocal
not
or
pass
raise
return
try
while
with
yield

C:\MyScripts>_
```

The first item on the Python search path is your current directory – so any file within there, or within any subdirectories you make there, will be found by the Python interpreter.

Spend a little time with the Interactive Mode help utility to discover lots more about Python.

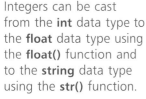

Integers can be cast from the **int** data type to the **float** data type using the **float()** function and to the **string** data type using the **str()** function.

Performing mathematics

Python includes a "math" module that provides lots of methods you can use to perform mathematical procedures once imported.

The **math.ceil()** and **math.floor()** methods enable a program to perform rounding of a floating point value specified between their parentheses to the closest integer – **math.ceil()** rounds up and **math.floor()** rounds down but the value returned, although an integer, is a **float** data type rather than an **int** data type.

The **math.pow()** method requires two arguments to raise a specified value by a specified power. The **math.sqrt()** method, on the other hand, simply requires a single argument and returns the square root of that specified value. Both method results are returned as a numeric value of the **float** data type.

Typical trigonometry can be performed using methods from the math module too, such as **math.sin()**, **math.cosin()** and **math.tan()**.

Python also includes a "random" module that can be used to produce pseudo random numbers once imported into a program.

The **random.random()** method produces a single floating-point number between zero and 1.0. Perhaps more interestingly, the **random.sample()** method produces a list of elements selected at random from a sequence. This method requires two arguments to specify the sequence to select from, and the length of the list to be produced. As the **range()** function returns a sequence of numbers, this can be used to specify a sequence as the first argument to the **random.sample()** method – so it will randomly select numbers from that sequence to produce a list in which no numbers repeat.

maths.py

1 Start a new Python script by importing the "math" and "random" modules to make their features available
```
import math , random
```

2 Next, add statements to display two rounded values
```
print( 'Rounded Up 9.5:' , math.ceil( 9.5 ) )
print( 'Rounded Down 9.5:' , math.floor( 9.5 ) )
```

3 Now, add a statement to initialize a variable with an integer value
```
num = 4
```

...cont'd

4 Add statements to display the square and square root of the variable value
```
print( num , 'Squared:' , math.pow( num , 2 ) )
print( num , 'Square Root:' , math.sqrt( num ) )
```

5 Then, add a statement to produce a random list of six unique numbers between one and 59
```
nums = random.sample( range( 1, 59 ) , 6 )
```

6 Finally, add a statement to display the random list
```
print( 'Your Lucky Lotto Numbers Are:' , nums )
```

7 Save the file in your scripts directory, then open a Command prompt window there and run this program – to see math results and random samples

```
Command Prompt                                    —   □   ×

C:\MyScripts>python maths.py
Rounded Up 9.5: 10
Rounded Down 9.5: 9
4 Squared: 16.0
4 Square Root: 2.0
Your Lucky Lotto Numbers Are: [47, 48, 13, 46, 26, 8]

C:\MyScripts>python maths.py
Rounded Up 9.5: 10
Rounded Down 9.5: 9
4 Squared: 16.0
4 Square Root: 2.0
Your Lucky Lotto Numbers Are: [1, 25, 19, 16, 9, 54]

C:\MyScripts>python maths.py
Rounded Up 9.5: 10
Rounded Down 9.5: 9
4 Squared: 16.0
4 Square Root: 2.0
Your Lucky Lotto Numbers Are: [55, 36, 31, 18, 42, 48]

C:\MyScripts>python maths.py
Rounded Up 9.5: 10
Rounded Down 9.5: 9
4 Squared: 16.0
4 Square Root: 2.0
Your Lucky Lotto Numbers Are: [53, 43, 13, 10, 34, 56]

C:\MyScripts>_
```

All the math methods here return floating-point numbers of the **float** data type.

The list produced by **random.sample()** does not actually replace elements of the sequence but merely copies a sample, as its name says.

Calculating decimals

Python programs that attempt floating-point arithmetic can produce unexpected and inaccurate results because the floating-point numbers cannot accurately represent all decimal numbers.

inaccurate.py

 1 Start a new Python script by initializing two variables with floating-point values
```
item = 0.70
rate = 1.05
```

2 Next, initialize two more variables by attempting floating-point arithmetic with the first two variables
```
tax = item * rate
total = item + tax
```

3 Now, add statements to display variable values formatted to have two decimal places so trailing zeros are shown
```
print( 'Item:\t' , '%.2f' % item )
print( 'Tax:\t' , '%.2f' % tax )
print( 'Total:\t' , '%.2f' % total )
```

Hot tip

Here, the variable values are formatted using a string substitution technique to show two decimal places – described in more detail on page 100.

4 Save the file in your scripts directory, then open a Command Prompt window there and run the program – to see the output display an inaccurate addition

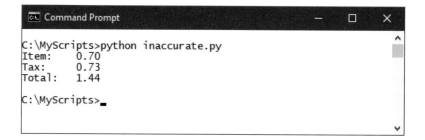

```
C:\MyScripts>python inaccurate.py
Item:    0.70
Tax:     0.73
Total:   1.44

C:\MyScripts>
```

expanded.py

5 To help understand this problem, edit all three print statements to display the variable values expanded to <u>20</u> decimal places, then run the modified program
```
print( 'Item:\t' , '%.20f' % item )
print( 'Tax:\t' , '%.20f' % tax )
print( 'Total:\t' , '%.20f' % total )
```

...cont'd

```
Command Prompt                                    —   □   ✕

C:\MyScripts>python expanded.py
Item:    0.69999999999999995559
Tax:     0.73499999999999998668
Total:   1.43500000000000005329

C:\MyScripts>_
```

It is now clear that the tax value is represented numerically slightly below 0.735, so gets rounded down to 0.73. Conversely, the total value is represented numerically slightly above 1.435, so gets rounded up to 1.44, creating the apparent addition error.

Errors in floating-point arithmetic can be avoided using Python's "decimal" module. This provides a **Decimal()** object with which floating-point numbers can be more accurately represented.

6 Add a statement at the beginning of the program to import the "decimal" module to make all features available
from decimal import *

7 Next, edit the first two variable assignment to objects
item = Decimal(0.70)
rate = Decimal(1.05)

8 Save the changes, then run the modified program to see both tax and total representations will now get rounded down – so the output will show accurate addition when string formatting is changed back to two decimal places

```
Command Prompt                                    —   □   ✕

C:\MyScripts>python decimals.py
Item:    0.70
Tax:     0.73
Total:   1.43

C:\MyScripts>_
```

This problem is not unique to Python – Java has a BigDecimal class that overcomes this problem in much the same way as the decimal module in Python.

decimals.py

Always use the **Decimal()** object to calculate monetary values or anywhere that accuracy is essential.

Telling the time

The Python "datetime" module can be imported into a program to make use of times and dates. It provides a **datetime** object with attributes of **year, month, day, hour, minute, second, microsecond**.

A **datetime** object has a **today()** method that assigns the current date and time values to its attributes and returns them in a tuple. It also has a **getattr()** method that requires two arguments specifying the datetime object name and attribute to retrieve. Alternatively, the attributes can be referenced using dot notation such as **datetime.year**.

All values in a **datetime** object are stored as numeric values but can, usefully, be transformed into text equivalents using its **strftime()** method. This requires a single string argument that is a "directive" specifying which part of the tuple to return and in what format. The possible directives are listed in the table below:

Hot tip

As the datetime object is in a module of the same name, simply importing the module means it would be referenced as **datetime.datetime**. Use **from datetime import *** so it can be referenced just as **datetime**.

Beware

As the **strftime()** method requires a string argument, the directive must be enclosed between quote marks.

Directive:	Returns:
%A	Full weekday name (%a for abbreviated day name)
%B	Full month name (%b for abbreviated month name)
%c	Date and time appropriate for locale
%d	Day of the month number 1-31
%f	Microsecond number 0-999999
%H	Hour number 0-23 (24-hour clock)
%I	Hour number 1-12 (12-hour clock)
%j	Day of the year number 0-366
%m	Month number 1-12
%M	Minute number 0-59
%p	AM or PM equivalent for locale
%S	Second number 0-59
%w	Week day number 0(Sunday)-6
%W	Week of the year number 0-53
%X	Time appropriate for locale (%x for appropriate date)
%Y	Year 0001-9999 (%y for year 00-99)
%z	Timezone offset from UTC as +HHMM or -HHMM
%Z	Timezone name

1 Start a new Python script by importing the "datetime" module to make its features available
from datetime import *

today.py

2 Next, create a datetime object with attributes assigned to current date and time values then display its contents
```
today = datetime.today()
print( 'Today Is:' , today )
```

3 Add a loop to display each attribute value individually
```
for attr in \
[ 'year','month','day','hour','minute','second','microsecond' ] :
        print( attr , ':\t' , getattr( today , attr ) )
```

Hot tip

Notice how the \ backslash character is used in this loop to allow a statement to continue on the next line without causing an error.

4 Now, add a statement to display time using dot notation
```
print( ' Time:' , today.hour , ':' , today.minute , sep = '' )
```

5 Then, assign formatted day and month names to variables
```
day = today.strftime( '%A' )
month = today.strftime( '%B' )
```

6 Finally, add a statement to display the formatted date
```
print( 'Date:' , day , month , today.day )
```

7 Save the file in your scripts directory, then open a Command Prompt window there and run this program – to see the date and time values get displayed

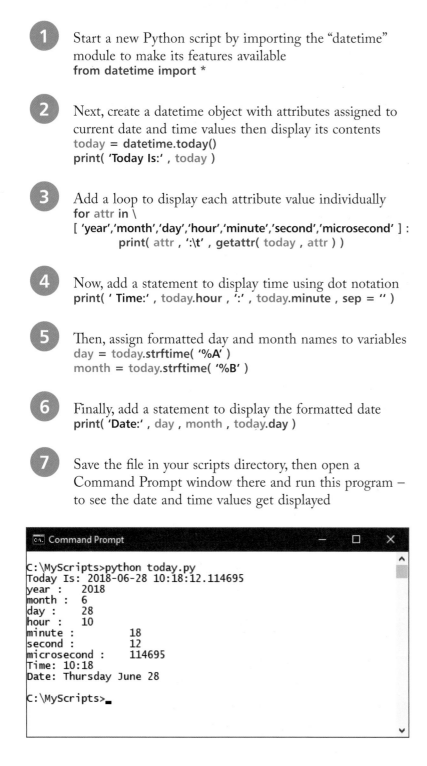

```
C:\MyScripts>python today.py
Today Is: 2018-06-28 10:18:12.114695
year :    2018
month :   6
day :     28
hour :    10
minute :          18
second :          12
microsecond :     114695
Time: 10:18
Date: Thursday June 28

C:\MyScripts>
```

Hot tip

You can assign new values to attributes of a datetime object using its **replace()** method, such as **today = today.replace(year=2020)**.

91

Running a timer

Getting the current time both before and after an event means that the duration of the event can be calculated by their difference. The Python "time" module can be imported into a program to provide various time-related functions.

Current system time is usually counted as the number of seconds elapsed since the Epoch at 00:00:00 GMT on January 1, 1970. The **time** module's **time()** method returns the current time in seconds since the Epoch as a floating point number when called.

The figure returned by the **time()** method can be converted into a "struct_time" object using **gmtime()** or **localtime()** methods. This object has attributes of **tm_year, tm_mon, tm_mday, tm_hour, tm_min, tm_sec, tm_wday, tm_yday, tm_yday** and **tm_isdst** that can be referenced using dot notation. For example, *struct*.**tm_wday**.

All values in a **struct_time** object are stored as numeric values but can be transformed into text equivalents using the **strftime()** method. This requires an argument that is a format "directive" followed by the name of the **struct_time** object. The possible directives include those listed in the table on page 90 for the **datetime** object. For example, **strftime('%A' , *struct*)** for weekday.

Usefully, the **time** module also provides a **sleep()** method that can be used to pause execution of a program. Its argument specifies the amount of time in seconds by which to delay execution.

The **gmtime()** method converts elapsed time from the Epoch to a **struct_time** object at UTC with the Daylight Saving Time always set to zero, whereas **localtime()** converts to a **struct_time** object at your local system time.

timer.py

 1 Start a new Python script by importing the "time" module to make its features available
from time import *

2 Next, initialize a variable with a floating point number that is the current elapsed time since the Epoch
start_timer = **time()**

3 Now, add a statement to create a **struct_time** object from the elapsed time value
struct = **localtime(** start_timer **)**

 4 Then, announce that a countdown timer is about to begin from the current time starting point
print('\nStarting Countdown At:' , strftime('%X' , struct))

...cont'd

5 Add a loop to initialize and print a counter variable value then decrement the counter by one and pause for one second on each iteration

```
i = 10
while i > -1 :
        print( i )
        i -= 1
        sleep( 1 )
```

6 Next, initialize a variable with a floating point number that is the current elapsed time now since the Epoch

```
end_timer = time()
```

7 Now, initialize a variable with the rounded seconds value of the time difference between the two timed points

```
difference = round( end_timer - start_timer )
```

8 Finally, add a statement to display the time taken to execute the countdown loop

```
print( '\nRuntime:' , difference , 'Seconds' )
```

9 Save the file in your scripts directory, then open a Command Prompt window there and run this program – to see the loop pause on each iteration and elapsed time

The argument to the **sleep()** method may be a floating point number to indicate a more precise sleep pause time.

Do not confuse the **time.strftime()** method used in this example with the **datetime.strftime()** method used in the previous example.

```
Command Prompt                          —   □   ×

C:\MyScripts>python timer.py

Starting Countdown At: 14:34:16
10
9
8
7
6
5
4
3
2
1
0

Runtime: 11 Seconds

C:\MyScripts>_
```

Matching patterns

The Python "re" module can be imported into a program to make use of Regular Expression patterns that describe a particular string of characters. Regular Expressions are useful for text validation and for search-and-replace operations within text by matching their specified pattern to a section of the text.

A Regular Expression pattern may consist entirely of "literal characters" describing a character string to match within some text. For example, the Regular Expression "wind" finds a match in "<u>wind</u>ows" – the pattern literally matches the string in the text. More typically, a Regular Expression pattern consists of a combination of literal characters and these "metacharacters":

Beware

The topic of Regular Expressions is extensive and beyond the remit of this book – but a brief introduction is provided here for completeness.

Metacharacter:	Matches:	Example:
.	**Any Characters**	py..on
^	**First Characters**	^ py
$	**Final Characters**	....on$
*	**Zero Or More Repetitions**	py*
+	**One Or More Repetitions**	py+
?	**Zero Or One Repetitions**	py?
{ }	**Multiple Repetitions**	a{ 3 }
[ ]	**Character Class**	[a-z]
\	**Special Sequence**	\s
|	**Either Optional Character**	a | b
( )	**Expression Group**	(...)

Don't forget

The character class **[a-z]** matches only lowercase characters, but **[a-z0-9]** also matches digits.

A combination of literals and metacharacters defining a pattern to be matched can be specified to the **re.compile()** method to return a pattern object. This object has a **match()** method to specify a string within its parentheses to compare against the pattern.

When a **match()** comparison succeeds, a match object is returned containing information about the match, otherwise a **None** value is returned when the comparison fails.

A match object has **start()** and **end()** methods, which return the position of the match, and a **group()** method that returns the string matched by the comparison.

...cont'd

1 Start a new Python script by importing the "re" module to make the regular expression methods available
from re import *

regex.py

2 Next, initialize a variable with a regular expression object
**pattern = \
compile('(^ |\s)[-a-z0-9_.]+@([-a-z0-9]+\.)+[a-z]{2,6}(\s|$)')**

3 Now, begin a function definition by requesting user input and attempt to match that with the pattern
**def get_address() :
        address = input('Enter Your Email Address: ')
        is_valid = pattern.match(address)**

4 Then, add indented statements to display an appropriate message describing whether the attempt succeeded
**   if is_valid :
                print('Valid Address:' , is_valid.group())
        else :
                print('Invalid Address! Please Retry...\n')**

5 Finally, add a statement to call the defined function
get_address()

6 Save the file in your scripts directory, then open a Command Prompt window there and run this program – to see that only a complete email address will validate

```
Command Prompt                                    —   □   ×

C:\MyScripts>python regex.py
Enter Your Email Address: mike
Invalid Address! Please Retry...

Enter Your Email Address: mike@
Invalid Address! Please Retry...

Enter Your Email Address: mike@example
Invalid Address! Please Retry...

Enter Your Email Address: mike@example.com
Valid Address: mike@example.com

C:\MyScripts>_
```

Hot tip

You can discover more about Regular Expressions in the Library Reference section of the Python documentation at **docs.python.org/3/library/re.html**

Summary

- Functions can be stored in modules that are named as the file name without the ".py" file extension.

- An **import** statement makes module functions available in a program by dot-suffixing their name after the module name.

- A **from import** statement makes module functions available in a program without the need to dot-suffix their name.

- The **sys** module has attributes that contain the Python version number, interpreter location, and path to search for modules.

- The **keyword** module has a **kwlist** attribute that contains a list of all current Python keywords.

- The **math** module provides methods to perform mathematical procedures such as **math.ceil()** and **math.floor()**.

- The **random** module provides a **random()** method that produces pseudo random numbers and a **sample()** method that produces a list of elements selected at random from a sequence.

- The **decimal** module provides a **Decimal()** object with which floating-point numbers can be accurately represented to calculate monetary values.

- The **datetime** module provides a **datetime** object with **year, month, day, hour, minute, second, microsecond** attributes that can be referenced by dot-suffixing or with the **getattr()** method.

- A **datetime** object has a **strftime()** method that can specify a directive to return a formatted part of the object.

- The **time** module provides a **time()** method that returns the current elapsed time in seconds since the Epoch.

- The **gmtime()** and **localtime()** methods return a struct_time object that has attributes containing date and time components.

- The **re** module provides a **compile()** method to create a Regular Expression pattern and a **match()** method to compare a pattern to a specified string.

6 Managing strings

This chapter demonstrates how to work with string data values and text files in Python programs.

Manipulating strings

String values can be manipulated in a Python program using the various operators listed in the table below:

Operator:	Description:	Example:
+	Concatenate – join strings together	'Hello' + 'Mike'
*	Repeat – multiply the string	'Hello' * 2
[ ]	Slice – select a character at a specified index position	'Hello' [0]
[:]	Range Slice – select characters in a specified index range	'Hello' [0 : 4]
in	Membership Inclusive – return True if character exists in the string	'H' in 'Hello'
not in	Membership Exclusive – return True if character doesn't exist in string	'h' not in 'Hello'
r/R	Raw String – suppress meaning of escape characters	print(r'\n')
''' '''	Docstring – describe a module, function, class, or method	def sum(a,b) : ''' Add Args '''

The [ ] slice operator and [:] range slice operator recognize that a string is simply a list containing an individual character within each list element, which can be referenced by their index number.

Similarly, the **in** and **not in** membership operators iterate through each element seeking to match the specified character.

The raw string operator **r** (or uppercase **R**) must be placed immediately before the opening quote mark to suppress escape characters in the string, and is useful when the string contains the backslash character.

A "docstring" is a descriptive string literal that occurs as the first statement in a module, a function, a class, or a method definition. This should be enclosed within triple single quote marks. Uniquely, the docstring becomes the **__doc__** special attribute of that object, so can be referenced using its name and dot-suffixing. All modules should normally have docstrings, and all functions and classes exported by a module should also have docstrings.

The membership operators perform a case-sensitive match, so **'A' in 'abc'** will fail.

The Range Slice returns the string up to, but not including, the final specified index position.

...cont'd

1 Start a new Python script by defining a simple function that includes a docstring description

```
def display( s ) :
        '''Display an argument value.'''
        print( s )
```

manipulate.py

2 Next, add a statement to display the function description

```
display( display.__doc__ )
```

3 Now, add a statement to display a raw string value that contains the backslash character

```
display( r'C:\Program Files' )
```

Beware

The **doc** keyword is preceded by TWO _ underscore characters and followed by TWO _ underscore characters.

4 Then, add a statement to display a concatenation of two string values that include an escape character and a space

```
display( '\nHello' + ' Python' )
```

5 Next, add a statement to display a slice of a specified string within a range of element index numbers

```
display( 'Python In Easy Steps\n' [ 7 : ] )
```

Don't forget

Remember that strings must be enclosed within either single quote marks or double quote marks.

6 Finally, display the results of seeking characters within a specified string

```
display( 'P' in 'Python' )
display( 'p' in 'Python' )
```

7 Save the file in your scripts directory, then open a Command Prompt window there and run this program – to see manipulated strings get displayed

```
C:\MyScripts>python manipulate.py
Display an argument value.
C:\Program Files

Hello Python
In Easy Steps

True
False

C:\MyScripts>_
```

Hot tip

With range slice, if the start index number is omitted, zero is assumed, and if the end index number is omitted, the string length is assumed.

Formatting strings

The Python built-in **dir()** function can be useful to examine the names of functions and variables defined in a module by specifying the module name within its parentheses. Interactive mode can easily be used for this purpose by importing the module name then calling the **dir()** function. The example below examines the "dog" module created on page 82 in the previous chapter:

Notice that the **__doc__** attribute introduced in the previous example appears listed here by the **dir()** function.

```
C:\MyScripts>python
Python 3.7.0
>>> import dog
>>> for i in dir( dog ) :
...      print( i )
...
__builtins__
__cached__
__doc__
__file__
__loader__
__name__
__package__
__spec__
bark
lick
nap
>>>
```

Those defined names that begin and end with a double underscore are Python objects, whereas the others are programmer-defined. The **__builtins__** module can also be examined using the **dir()** function, to examine the names of functions and variables defined by default, such as the **print()** function and a **str** object.

Do not confuse the **str** object described here with the **str()** function that converts values to the string data type.

The **str** object defines several useful methods for string formatting, including an actual **format()** method that performs replacements. A string to be formatted by the **format()** method can contain both text and "replacement fields" marking places where text is to be inserted from an ordered comma-separated list of values. Each replacement field is denoted by **{ }** braces, which may, optionally, contain the index number position of the replacement in the list.

Strings may also be formatted using the C-style **%s** substitution operator to mark places in a string where text is to be inserted from a comma-separated ordered list of values.

...cont'd

1 Start a new Python script by initializing a variable with a formatted string
```
snack = '{} and {}'.format( 'Burger' , 'Fries' )
```

2 Next, display the variable value to see the text replaced in their listed order
```
print( '\nReplaced:' , snack )
```

3 Now, assign a differently-formatted string to the variable
```
snack = '{1} and {0}'.format( 'Burger' , 'Fries' )
```

4 Then, display the variable value again to see the text now replaced by their specified index element value
```
print( 'Replaced:' , snack )
```

5 Assign another formatted string to the variable
```
snack = '%s and %s' % ( 'Milk' , 'Cookies' )
```

6 Finally, display the variable value once more to see the text substituted in their listed order
```
print( '\nSubstituted:' , snack )
```

7 Save the file in your scripts directory, then open a Command Prompt window there and run this program – to see formatted strings get displayed

format.py

Beware

You cannot leave spaces around the index number in the replacement field.

101

Hot tip

Other data types can be substituted using **%d** for a decimal integer, **%c** for a character, and **%f** for a floating-point number.

```
Command Prompt                          —   □   ×

C:\MyScripts>python format.py

Replaced: Burger and Fries
Replaced: Fries and Burger

Substituted: Milk and Cookies

C:\MyScripts>_
```

Modifying strings

The Python **str** object has many useful methods that can be dot-suffixed to its name for modification of the string and to examine its contents. The most commonly used string modification methods are listed in the table below, together with a brief description:

Method:	Description:
capitalize( )	Change string's first letter to uppercase
title( )	Change all first letters to uppercase
upper( ) lower( ) swapcase( )	Change the case of all letters to uppercase, to lowercase, or to the inverse of the current case respectively
join(*seq*)	Merge string into separator sequence *seq*
lstrip( ) rstrip ( ) strip( )	Remove leading whitespace, trailing whitespace, or both leading and trailing whitespace respectively
replace(*old* , *new*)	Replace all occurrences of *old* with *new*
ljust(*w* , *c*) rjust(*w* , *c*)	Pad string to right or left respectively to total column width *w* with character *c*
center(*w* , *c*)	Pad string each side to total column width *w* with character *c* (default is space)
count(*sub*)	Return the number of occurrences of *sub*
find(*sub*)	Return the index number of the first occurrence of *sub* or return -1 if not found
startswith(*sub*) endswith(*sub*)	Return True if *sub* is found at start or end respectively – otherwise return False
isalpha( ) isnumeric( ) isalnum( )	Return True if all characters are letters only, are numbers only, or are letters or numbers only – otherwise return False
islower( ) isupper( ) istitle( )	Return True if string characters are lowercase, uppercase, or all first letters are uppercase only – otherwise return False
isspace( )	Return True if string contains only whitespace – otherwise return False
isdigit( ) isdecimal( )	Return True if string contains only digits or decimals – otherwise return False

Beware

A space character is not alphanumeric so **isalnum()** returns **False** when examining strings that contain spaces.

102

1 Start a new Python script by initializing a variable with a string of lowercase characters and spaces
```
string = 'python in easy steps'
```

modify.py

2 Next, display the string capitalized, titled, and centered
```
print( '\nCapitalized:\t' , string.capitalize() )
print( '\nTitled:\t\t' , string.title() )
print( '\nCentered:\t' , string.center( 30 , '*' ) )
```

3 Now, display the string in all uppercase and merged with a sequence of two asterisks
```
print( '\nUppercase:\t' , string.upper() )
print( '\nJoined:\t\t' , string.join( '**' ) )
```

4 Then, display the string padded with asterisks on the left
```
print( '\nJustified:\t' ,string.rjust( 30 , '*' ) )
```

5 Finally, display the string with all occurrences of the 's' character replaced by asterisks
```
print( '\nReplaced:\t' , string.replace( 's' , '*' ) )
```

6 Save the file in your scripts directory, then open a Command Prompt window there and run this program – to see modified strings get displayed

```
Command Prompt                                   —    □    ×

C:\MyScripts>python modify.py

Capitalized:       Python in easy steps

Titled:            Python In Easy Steps

Centered:          *****python in easy steps*****

Uppercase:         PYTHON IN EASY STEPS

Joined:            *python in easy steps*

Justified:         **********python in easy steps

Replaced:          python in ea*y *tep*

C:\MyScripts>
```

Don't forget

With the **rjust()** method a RIGHT-justified string gets padding added to its LEFT, and with the **ljust()** method a LEFT-justified string gets padding added to its RIGHT.

103

Converting strings

Before Python 3.0, string characters were stored by their ASCII numeric code values in the range 0-127, representing only un-accented Latin characters. For example, the lowercase letter 'a' is assigned 97 as its code value. Each byte of computer memory can, in fact, store values in the range 0-255 but this is still too limited to represent all accented characters and non-Latin characters. For example, accented characters used in Western Europe and the Cyrillic alphabet used for Russian cannot be represented in the range 128-255 because there are more than 127 such characters. Recent versions of Python overcome this limitation by storing string characters as their Unicode code point value to represent all characters and alphabets in the numeric range 0-1,114,111. Characters that are above the ASCII range may require two bytes for their code point value, such as hexadecimal **0xC3 0xB6** for 'ö'.

The **str** object's **encode()** method can be used to convert from the default Unicode encoding, and its **decode()** method can be used to convert back to the Unicode default encoding.

Python's "unicodedata" module, usefully, provides a **name()** method that reveals the Unicode name of each character. Accented and non-Latin characters can be referenced by their Unicode name or by decoding their Unicode hexadecimal code point value.

Hot tip

The term "ASCII" is an acronym for American Standard Code for Information Interchange.

unicode.py

 Start a new Python script by initializing a variable with a string containing a non-ASCII character then display its value, data type, and string length
```
s = 'Röd'
print( '\nRed String:' , s )
print( 'Type:' , type( s ) , '\tLength:' , len( s ) )
```

 Next, encode the string and again display its value, data type, and string length
```
s = s.encode( 'utf-8' )
print( '\nEncoded String:' , s )
print( 'Type:' , type( s ) , '\tLength:' , len( s ) )
```

 Now, decode the string and once more display its value, data type, and string length – to reveal the hexadecimal code point of the non-ASCII character
```
s = s.decode( 'utf-8' )
print( '\nDecoded String:' , s )
print( 'Type:' , type( s ) , '\tLength:' , len( s ) )
```

4 Then, add statements to make "unicodedata" features available and a loop to reveal the Unicode name of each character in the string

```
import unicodedata
for i in range( len( s ) ) :
        print( s[ i ] , unicodedata.name( s[ i ] ) , sep = ' : ' )
```

5 Next, add statements to assign the variable a new value that includes a hexadecimal code point for a non-ASCII character then display the decoded string value

```
s = b'Gr\xc3\xb6n'
print( '\nGreen String:' , s.decode( 'utf-8' ) )
```

A string containing byte addresses must be immediately prefixed by a **b** to denote that string as a byte literal.

6 Finally, add statements to assign the variable another new value that includes a Unicode character name for a non-ASCII character then display the string value

```
s = 'Gr\N{LATIN SMALL LETTER O WITH DIAERESIS}n'
print( 'Green String:' , s )
```

7 Save the file in your scripts directory, then open a Command Prompt window there and run this program – to see converted strings and unicode character names

```
C:\MyScripts>python unicode.py

Red String: Röd
Type: <class 'str'>        Length: 3

Encoded String: b'R\xc3\xb6d'
Type: <class 'bytes'>      Length: 4

Decoded String: Röd
Type: <class 'str'>        Length: 3
R : LATIN CAPITAL LETTER R
ö : LATIN SMALL LETTER O WITH DIAERESIS
d : LATIN SMALL LETTER D

Green String: Grön
Green String: Grön

C:\MyScripts>_
```

Unicode names are uppercase and referenced by inclusion between **{ }** braces prefixed by a **\N** in this notation format.

Accessing files

The **__builtins__** module can be examined using the **dir()** function to reveal that it contains a **file** object that defines several methods for working with files, including **open()**, **read()**, **write()**, and **close()**.

Before a file can be read or written, it firstly must always be opened using the **open()** method. This requires two string arguments to specify the name and location of the file, and one of the following "mode" specifiers in which to open the file:

Beware

File mode arguments are string values so must be surrounded by quotes.

File mode:	Operation:
r	Open an existing file to read
w	Open an existing file to write. Creates a new file if none exists, or opens an existing file and discards all its previous contents
a	Append text. Opens or creates a text file for writing at the end of the file
r+	Open a text file to read from or write to
w+	Open a text file to write to or read from
a+	Open or creates a text file to read from or write to at the end of the file

Where the mode includes a **b** after any of the file modes listed above, the operation relates to a binary file rather than a text file. For example, **rb** or **w+b**

Once a file is opened and you have a **file** object, you can get various details related to that file from its properties:

Hot tip

You can also use a **readlines()** method that returns a list of all lines.

Property:	Description:
name	Name of the opened file
mode	Mode in which the file was opened
closed	Status Boolean value of **True** or **False**
readable( )	Read permission Boolean value of **True** or **False**
writable( )	Write permission Boolean value of **True** or **False**

1 Start a new Python script by creating a file object for a new text file named "example.txt" to write content into
```
file = open( 'example.txt' , 'w' )
```

access.py

2 Next, add statements to display the file name and mode
```
print( 'File Name:' , file.name )
print( 'File Open Mode:' , file.mode )
```

3 Now, add statements to display the file access permissions
```
print( 'Readable:' , file.readable() )
print( 'Writable:' , file.writable() )
```

4 Then, define a function to determine the file's status
```
def get_status( f ) :
        if ( f.closed != False ) :
                return 'Closed'
        else :
                return 'Open'
```

5 Finally, add statements to display the current file status then close the file and display the file status once more
```
print( 'File Status:' , get_status( file ) )
file.close()
print( '\nFile Status:' , get_status( file ) )
```

6 Save the file in your scripts directory, then open a Command Prompt window there and run this program – to see a file get opened for writing then get closed

```
C:\MyScripts>python access.py
File Name: example.txt
File Open Mode: w
Readable: False
Writable: True
File Status: Open

File Status: Closed

C:\MyScripts>
```

Don't forget

If your program tries to open a non-existent file in **r** mode, the interpreter will report an error.

107

Reading and writing files

Once a file has been successfully opened it can be read or added to, or new text can be written in the file, depending on the mode specified in the call to the **open()** method. Following this, the open file must then always be closed by calling the **close()** method.

As you might expect, the **read()** method returns the entire content of the file, and the **write()** method adds content to the file.

You can quickly and efficiently read the entire contents in a loop, iterating line by line.

file.py

 Start a new Python script by initializing a variable with a concatenated string containing newline characters
```
poem = 'I never saw a man who looked\n'
poem += 'With such a wistful eye\n'
poem += 'Upon that little tent of blue\n'
poem += 'Which prisoners call the sky\n'
```

 Next, add a statement to create a file object for a new text file named "poem.txt" to write content into
```
file = open( 'poem.txt' , 'w' )
```

 Now, add statements to write the string contained in the variable into the text file, then close that file
```
file.write( poem )
file.close()
```

Beware

Writing to an existing file will automatically overwrite its contents!

4 Then, add a statement to create a file object for the existing text file "poem.txt" to read from
```
file = open( 'poem.txt' , 'r' )
```

 Now, add statements to display the contents of the text file, then close that file
```
for line in file :
        print( line , end = '' )
file.close()
```

6 Save the file in your scripts directory, then open a Command Prompt window there and run this program – to see the file get created then read out to display

108

```
C:\MyScripts>python file.py
I never saw a man who looked
With such a wistful eye
Upon that little tent of blue
Which prisoners call the sky

C:\MyScripts>notepad poem.txt

C:\MyScripts>
```

Hot tip

Suppress the default newline provided by the **print()** function where the strings themselves contain newlines.

7 Launch the Notepad text editor to confirm the new text file exists and reveal its contents written by the program

```
poem.txt - Notepad
File  Edit  Format  View  Help
I never saw a man who looked
With such a wistful eye
Upon that little tent of blue
Which prisoners call the sky
```

8 Now, add statements at the end of the program to append a citation to the text file then save the script file again

```python
file = open( 'poem.txt' , 'a' )
file.write( '(Oscar Wilde)' )
file.close()
```

Hot tip

You can also use the file object's **readlines()** method that returns a list of all lines in a file – one line per element.

9 Run this program again to re-write the text file then view its contents in Notepad – to see the citation now appended after the original text content

```
poem.txt - Notepad
File  Edit  Format  View  Help
I never saw a man who looked
With such a wistful eye
Upon that little tent of blue
Which prisoners call the sky
(Oscar Wilde)
```

Updating file strings

A file object's **read()** method will, by default, read the entire contents of the file from the very beginning, at index position zero, to the very end – at the index position of the final character. Optionally, the **read()** method can accept an integer argument to specify how many characters it should read.

The position within the file, from which to read or at which to write, can be finely controlled using the file object's **seek()** method. This accepts an integer argument specifying how many characters to move position as an offset from the start of the file.

The current position within a file can be discovered at any time by calling the file object's **tell()** method to return an integer location.

When working with file objects it is good practice to use the Python **with** keyword to group the file operational statements within a block. This technique ensures that the file is properly closed after operations end, even if an exception is raised on the way, and is much shorter than writing equivalent **try except** blocks.

update.py

 Start a new Python script by assigning a string value to a variable containing text to be written in a file
text = 'The political slogan "Workers Of The World Unite!" is from The Communist Manifesto.'

 Next, add statements to write the text string into a file and display the file's current status in the "with" block
```
with open( 'update.txt' , 'w' ) as file :
        file.write( text )
        print( '\nFile Now Closed?:' , file.closed )
```

3 Now, add a non-indented statement after the "with" code block to display the file's new status
```
print( 'File Now Closed?:' , file.closed )
```

 Then, re-open the file and display its contents to confirm it now contains the entire text string
```
with open( 'update.txt' , 'r+' ) as file :
        text = file.read()
        print( '\nString:' , text )
```

5 Next, add indented statements to display the current file position, then reposition and display that new position

```
print( '\nPosition In File Now:' , file.tell() )
position = file.seek( 33 )
print( 'Position In File Now:' , file.tell() )
```

6 Now, add an indented statement to overwrite the text from the current file position

```
file.write( 'All Lands' )
```

7 Then, add indented statements to reposition in the file once more and overwrite the text from the new position

```
file.seek( 59 )
file.write( 'the tombstone of Karl Marx.' )
```

8 Finally, add indented statements to return to the start of the file and display its entire updated contents

```
file.seek( 0 )
text = file.read()
print( '\nString:' , text )
```

9 Save the file to your scripts directory, then open a Command Prompt window there and run this program – to see the file strings get updated

```
C:\MyScripts>python update.py

File Now Closed?: False
File Now Closed?: True

String: The political slogan "Workers Of The World Unite!"
is from The Communist Manifesto.

Position In File Now: 83
Position In File Now: 33

String: The political slogan "Workers Of All Lands Unite!"
is from the tombstone of Karl Marx.

C:\MyScripts>_
```

The **seek()** method may, optionally, accept a second argument value of **0**, **1**, or **2** to move the specified number of characters from the start, current, or end position respectively – zero is the default start position.

As with strings, the first character in a file is at index position zero – not at index position one.

Pickling data

In Python, string data can easily be stored in text files using the techniques demonstrated in the previous examples. Other data types, such as numbers, lists, or dictionaries, could also be stored in text files but would require conversion to strings first. Restoring that stored data to their original data type on retrieval would require another conversion. An easier way to achieve data persistence of any data object is provided by the "pickle" module.

The process of "pickling" objects stores a string representation of an object that can later be "unpickled" to its former state, and is a very common Python programming procedure.

An object can be converted for storage in a file by specifying the object and file as arguments to the **pickle** object's **dump()** method. It can later be restored from that file by specifying the file name as the sole argument to the **pickle** object's **load()** method.

Unless the storage file needs to be human-readable for some reason, it is more efficient to use a machine-readable binary file.

Where the program needs to check for the existence of a storage file, the "os" module provides a **path** object with an **isfile()** method that returns **True** if a file specified within its parentheses is found.

data.py

1 Start a new Python script by making "pickle" and "os" module methods available
import pickle , os

2 Next, add a statement to test that a specific data file does not already exist
if not os.path.isfile('pickle.dat') :

3 Now, add a statement to create a list of two elements if the specified file is not found
data = [0 , 1]

4 Then, add statements to request user data to be assigned to each of the list elements
data[0] = input('Enter Topic: ')
data[1] = input('Enter Series: ')

5 Next, add a statement to create a binary file for writing to

```
file = open( 'pickle.dat' , 'wb' )
```

6 Now, add a statement to dump the values contained in the variables as data into the binary file

```
pickle.dump( data , file )
```

7 Then, after writing the file remember to close it

```
file.close()
```

Pickling is the standard way to create Python objects that can be used in other programs.

8 Next, add alternative statements to open an existing file to read from if a specific data file does already exist

```
else :
    file = open( 'pickle.dat' , 'rb' )
```

9 Now, add statements to load the data stored in that existing file into a variable then close the file

```
data = pickle.load( file )
file.close()
```

10 Finally, add a statement to display the restored data

```
print( '\nWelcome Back To:' , data[ 0 ] , data[ 1 ] )
```

11 Save the file in your scripts directory, then open a Command prompt window there and run this program – to see user input get stored in a file then get retrieved

Although this example just stores two string values in a list, pickling can store almost any type of Python object.

```
C:\MyScripts>python data.py

Enter Topic: Python
Enter Series: In Easy Steps

C:\MyScripts>python data.py

Welcome Back To: Python In Easy Steps

C:\MyScripts>_
```

Summary

- Strings can be manipulated by operators for concatenation **+**, selecting slices **[ ]**, and membership with **in** and **not in**.

- The special **__doc__** attribute can contain a "docstring" describing a module, function, class, or method.

- Python's built-in **dir()** function can be useful to examine the names of functions and variables defined in a module.

- The **__builtins__** module contains functions and variables that are available by default, such as the **print()** function.

- A **str** object has a **format()** method for string formatting, and many methods for string modification, such as **capitalize()**.

- Unicode character encoding is used by default, but this can be changed with the **str** object's **encode()** and **decode()** methods.

- The **unicodedata** module provides a **name()** method that reveals the Unicode name of each character.

- A file object has **open()**, **read()**, **write()**, and **close()** methods for working with files, and features that describe the file properties.

- The **open()** method must specify a file name string argument and a file mode string argument, such as **'r'** to read the file.

- Position in a file, at which to read or write, can be specified with the **seek()** method and reported by the **tell()** method.

- The Python **with** keyword groups file operational statements within a block and automatically closes an open file.

- The process of "pickling" objects stores a string representation of an object that can later be "unpickled" to its former state.

- A **pickle** object's **dump()** method requires arguments to specify an object for conversion, and a file name in which to store data.

- Stored object data can be retrieved by specifying the file name in which it is stored to the **pickle** object's **load()** method.

7 Programming objects

This chapter demonstrates how to use Python for Object Oriented Programming.

Encapsulating data

A "class" is a specified prototype describing a set of properties that characterize an object. Each class has a data structure that can contain both functions and variables to characterize the object.

The properties of a class are referred to as its data "members". Class function members are known as its "methods", and class variable members (declared within a class structure but outside any method definitions) are known as its "attributes".

Class members can be referenced throughout a program using dot notation, suffixing the member name after the class name, with syntax of **class-name.method-name()** or **class-name.attribute-name**.

A class declaration begins with the **class** keyword, followed by a programmer-specified name (adhering to the usual Python naming conventions but beginning in uppercase) then a : colon. Next, come indented statements optionally specifying a class document string, class variable attribute declarations, and class method definitions – so the class block syntax looks like this:

class ClassName :

    '' class-documentation-string '''

    class-variable-declarations

    class-method-definitions

The class declaration, which specifies its attributes and methods, is a blueprint from which working copies ("instances") can be made.

All variables declared within method definitions are known as "instance" variables and are only available locally within the method in which they are declared – they cannot be directly referenced outside the class structure.

Typically, instance variables contain data passed by the caller when an instance copy of the class is created. As this data is only available locally for internal use, it is effectively hidden from the rest of the program. This technique of data "encapsulation" ensures that data is securely stored within the class structure and is the first principle of Object Oriented Programming (OOP).

Hot tip

It is conventional to begin class names with an uppercase character, and object names with lowercase.

All properties of a class are referenced internally by the dot notation prefix **self** – so an attribute named "sound" is **self.sound**. Additionally, all method definitions in a class must have **self** as their first argument – so a method named "talk" is **talk(self)**.

When a class instance is created, a special **__init__(self)** method is automatically called. Subsequent arguments can be added in its parentheses if values are to be passed to initialize its attributes.

A complete Python class declaration could look like this example:

```
class Critter :

        ''' A base class for all critter properties. '''

        count = 0

        def __init__( self , chat ) :

                self.sound = chat
                Critter.count += 1

        def talk( self ) :

                return self.sound
```

It is useful to examine the class components of this example:

● The variable **count** is a class variable whose integer value gets shared among all instances of this class – this value can be referenced as **Critter.count** from inside or outside the class.

● The first method **__init__()** is the initialization method that is automatically called when an instance of the class is created.

● The **__init__()** method in this case initializes an instance variable **sound**, with a value passed from the **chat** argument, and increments the value of the **count** class variable whenever an instance of this class is created.

● The second method **talk()** is declared like a regular function, except the first argument is **self**, which is automatically incorporated – no value needs to be passed from the caller.

● The **talk()** method in this case simply returns the value encapsulated in the **sound** instance variable.

The class documentation string can be accessed via the special **__doc__** docstring attribute with *Classname.__doc__* .

While a program class cannot perfectly emulate a real-word object, the aim is to encapsulate all relevant attributes and actions.

Creating instance objects

An "instance" of a class object is simply a copy of the prototype created by calling that class name's constructor and specifying the required number of arguments within its parentheses. The call's arguments must match those specified by the **_init_()** method definition – other than a value for the internal **self** argument.

The class instance object returned by the constructor is assigned to a variable using the syntax *instance-name = ClassName(args)*.

Dot notation can be used to reference the methods and class variable attributes of an instance object by suffixing their name as *instance-name.method-name()* or *instance-name.attribute-name*.

Typically, a base class can be defined as a Python module file so it can be imported into other scripts where instance objects can be easily created from the "master" class prototype.

 1 Start a new Python script by declaring a new class with a descriptive document string
class Bird :

> **'''A base class to define bird properties.'''**

 2 Next, add an indented statement to declare and initialize a class variable attribute with an integer zero value
count = 0

 3 Now, define the initializer class method to initialize an instance variable and to increment the class variable
def _init_(self , chat) :

> **self.sound = chat**
> **Bird.count += 1**

 4 Finally, add a class method to return the value of the instance variable when called – then save this class file
def talk(self) :

> **return self.sound**

5 Start another Python script by making features of the class file available, then display its document string
from Bird import *
print('\nClass Instances Of:\n' , Bird.__doc__)

instance.py

6 Next, add a statement to create an instance of the class and pass a string argument value to its instance variable
polly = Bird('Squawk, squawk!')

7 Now, display this instance variable value and call the class method to display the common class variable value
print('\nNumber Of Birds:' , polly.count)
print('Polly Says:' , polly.talk())

Bird instance - polly

8 Create a second instance of the class, passing a different string argument value to its instance variable
harry = Bird('Tweet, tweet!')

9 Finally, display this instance variable value and call the class method to display the common class variable value
print('\nNumber Of Birds:' , harry.count)
print('Harry Says:' , harry.talk())

Bird instance - harry

10 Save the file in your scripts directory, then open a Command Prompt window there and run this program – to see two instances of the Bird class get created

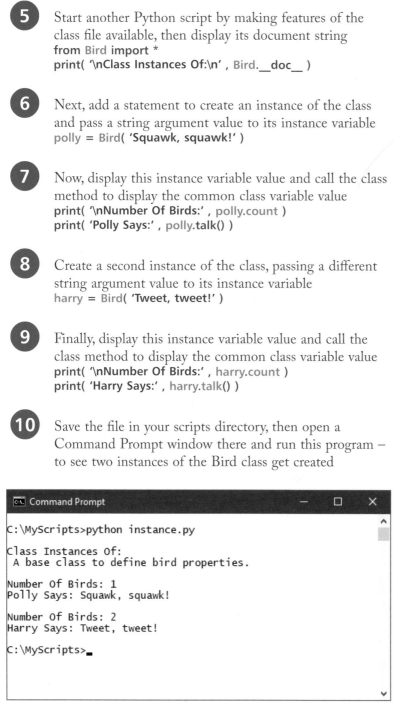

```
C:\MyScripts>python instance.py

Class Instances Of:
 A base class to define bird properties.

Number Of Birds: 1
Polly Says: Squawk, squawk!

Number Of Birds: 2
Harry Says: Tweet, tweet!

C:\MyScripts>
```

119

The class variable **count** can also be referenced with **Bird.count**, but the encapsulated instance variable **sound** can only be accessed by calling an instance's **talk()** method.

Addressing class attributes

An attribute of a class instance can be added, modified, or removed at any time using dot notation to address the attribute. Making a statement that assigns a value to an attribute will update the value contained within an existing attribute or create a new attribute of the specified name containing the assigned value:

instance-name.attribute-name = *value*
del *instance-name.attribute-name*

Alternatively, you can use the following Python built-in functions to add, modify, or remove an instance variable:

- **getattr(** *instance-name* , *'attribute-name'* **)** – return the attribute value of the class instance.

- **hasattr(** *instance-name* , *'attribute-name'* **)** – return **True** if the attribute value exists in the instance, otherwise return **False**.

- **setattr(** *instance-name* , *'attribute-name'* , *value* **)** – update the existing attribute value or create a new attribute in the instance.

- **delattr(** *instance-name* , *'attribute-name'* **)** – remove the attribute from the instance.

The name of attributes automatically supplied by Python always begin with an underscore character to notionally indicate "privacy" – so these should not be modified, or removed. You can add your own attributes named in this way to indicate privacy if you wish, but in reality these can be modified like any other attribute.

Beware

The attribute name specified to these built-in functions must be enclosed within quotes.

PY

address.py

1 Start a new Python script by making features of the Bird class available that was created on page 118
from Bird import *

2 Next, create an instance of the class, then add a new attribute with an assigned value using dot notation
chick = Bird('Cheep, cheep!')
chick.age = '1 week'

3 Now, display the values in both instance variable attributes
print('\nChick Says:' , chick.talk())
print('Chick Age:' , chick.age)

4 Then, modify the new attribute using dot notation and display its new value

```
chick.age = '2 weeks'
print( 'Chick Now:' , chick.age )
```

Bird instance - chick

5 Next, modify the new attribute once more, this time using a built-in function

```
setattr( chick , 'age' , '3 weeks' )
```

6 Now, display a list of all non-private instance attributes and their respective values using a built-in function

```
print( '\nChick Attributes...' )
for attrib in dir( chick ) :
        if attrib[0] != '_' :
                print( attrib , ':' , getattr( chick , attrib ) )
```

7 Finally, remove the new attribute and confirm its removal using a built-in function

```
delattr( chick , 'age' )
print( '\nChick age Attribute?' , hasattr( chick , 'age' ) )
```

This loop skips any attribute whose name begins with an underscore, so "private" attributes will not get displayed in the list.

8 Save the file in your scripts directory, then open a Command Prompt window there and run this program – to see the instance attributes get addressed

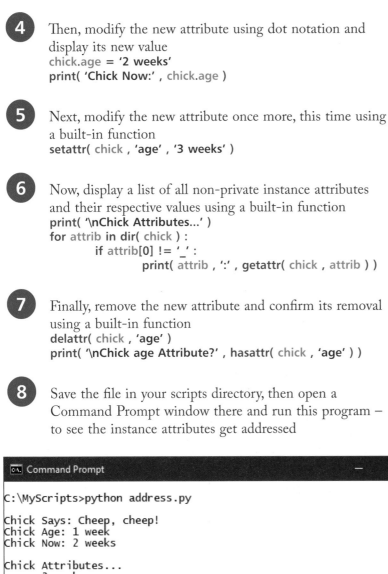

```
C:\MyScripts>python address.py

Chick Says: Cheep, cheep!
Chick Age: 1 week
Chick Now: 2 weeks

Chick Attributes...
age : 3 weeks
count : 1
sound : Cheep, cheep!
talk : <bound method Bird.talk of <Bird.Bird object at 0x012EEBD0>>

Chick age Attribute? False

C:\MyScripts>
```

Examining built-in attributes

Each Python class is automatically created with a number of built-in private attributes whose values can be referenced using dot notation. For example, with **class-name.__doc__** to see the document string attribute value of a specified class name.

The built-in **dir()** function can be used to display a list of all the built-in attributes in a class specified within its parentheses by testing whether each attribute name begins with an underscore.

The built-in **__dict__** attribute contains a "namespace" dictionary of class component keys and their associated values. The dictionary of a base class includes its default **__init__()** method, and all class methods and attributes. The dictionary of a class instance includes its instance attributes.

builtin.py

 1 Start a new Python script by making features of the Bird class available that was created on page 118
from Bird import *

 2 Next, add a statement to create an instance of the class
zola = Bird('Beep, beep!')

3 Now, add a loop to display all built-in instance attributes
print('\nBuilt-in Instance Attributes...')
for attrib in dir(zola) :
        if attrib[0] == '_' :
               print(attrib)

 4 Then, add a loop to display all items in the class dictionary
print('\nClass Dictionary...')
for item in Bird.__dict__ :
        print(item , ':' , Bird.__dict__[item])

5 Finally, add a loop to display all items in the instance dictionary
print('\nInstance Dictionary...')
for item in zola.__dict__ :
        print(item , ':' , zola.__dict__[item])

 6 Save the file in your scripts directory, then open a Command Prompt window there and run this program – to examine the built-in attributes

The function values stored in the dictionary are the machine addresses where the functions are stored.

```
C:\MyScripts>python builtin.py

Built-in Instance Attributes...
__class__
__delattr__
__dict__
__dir__
__doc__
__eq__
__format__
__ge__
__getattribute__
__gt__
__hash__
__init__
__init_subclass__
__le__
__lt__
__module__
__ne__
__new__
__reduce__
__reduce_ex__
__repr__
__setattr__
__sizeof__
__str__
__subclasshook__
__weakref__

Class Dictionary...
__module__ : Bird
__doc__ : A base class to define bird properties.
count : 1
__init__ : <function Bird.__init__ at 0x02F088A0>
talk : <function Bird.talk at 0x02F088E8>
__dict__ : <attribute '__dict__' of 'Bird' objects>
__weakref__ : <attribute '__weakref__' of 'Bird' objects>

Instance Dictionary...
sound : Beep, beep!

C:\MyScripts>_
```

Bird - zola.

A class instance is first created in this program so the __init__() method has been called to increment the **count** value before the dictionary gets listed.

The class dictionary output displays all class attributes, whereas the instance dictionary output displays only instance attributes – the class attributes are shared by the instance.

The **__weakref__** attribute is simply used internally for automatic garbage collection of "weak references" in the program for efficiency.

Collecting garbage

When a class instance object is created it is allocated a unique memory address that can be seen using the built-in **id()** function. Python automatically performs "garbage collection" to free up memory space by periodically deleting un-needed objects such as class instances – so their memory address becomes vacant.

Whenever an object gets assigned a new name or gets placed in a container, such as a list, its "reference count" increases. Conversely, whenever these are removed or go out of scope its count decreases. The object becomes eligible for collection when this count is zero.

Destroying an instance of a class may, optionally, call upon a "destructor" to execute a **__del__()** method – explicitly reclaiming occupied memory space and executing any specified statements.

Songbird.py

 1 Start a new Python script by declaring a class with an initializer method creating two instance variables and a method to display one of those variable values
```
class Songbird :
        def __init__( self , name , song ) :
                self.name = name
                self.song = song
                print( self.name , 'Is Born...' )
```

 2 Next, add a method to simply display both variable values
```
        def sing( self ) :
                print( self.name , 'Sings:' , self.song )
```

3 Now, add a destructor method for confirmation when instances of the class are destroyed – then save this file
```
        def __del__( self ) :
                print( self.name , 'Flew Away!\n' )
```

garbage.py

4 Start another Python script by making features of the class file available
```
from Songbird import *
```

5 Next, create an instance of the class, then display its instance attribute values and its identity address
```
bird_1 = Songbird( 'Koko' , 'Tweet, tweet!\n' )
print( bird_1.name , 'ID:' , id( bird_1 ) )
bird_1.sing()
```

Now, delete this instance – calling its destructor method
`del bird_1`

Songbird - Koko

 Create two more instances of the class, then display their
instance attribute values and their identity addresses
```
bird_2 = Songbird( 'Louie' , 'Chirp, chirp!\n' )
print( bird_2.name , 'ID:' , id( bird_2 ) )
bird_2.sing()

bird_3 = Songbird( 'Misty' , 'Squawk, squawk!\n' )
print( bird_3.name , 'ID:' , id( bird_3 ) )
bird_3.sing()
```

Songbird - Louie

 Finally, delete these instances – calling their destructors
```
del bird_2
del bird_3
```

Songbird - Misty

Save the file in your scripts directory, then open a
Command Prompt window there and run this program –
to see memory space handled by garbage collection

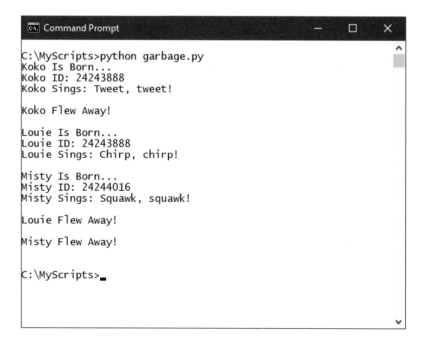

```
C:\MyScripts>python garbage.py
Koko Is Born...
Koko ID: 24243888
Koko Sings: Tweet, tweet!

Koko Flew Away!

Louie Is Born...
Louie ID: 24243888
Louie Sings: Chirp, chirp!

Misty Is Born...
Misty ID: 24244016
Misty Sings: Squawk, squawk!

Louie Flew Away!

Misty Flew Away!

C:\MyScripts>_
```

125

The second instance
created here is allocated
the memory address
vacated when the first
instance was deleted.

Inheriting features

A Python class can be created as a brand new class, like those in previous examples, or can be "derived" from an existing class. Importantly, a derived class inherits members of the parent (base) class from which it is derived – in addition to its own members.

The ability to inherit members from a base class allows derived classes to be created that share certain common properties, which have been defined in the base class. For example, a "Polygon" base class may define width and height properties that are common to all polygons. Classes of "Rectangle" and Triangle" could be derived from the Polygon class – inheriting width and height properties, in addition to their own members defining their unique features.

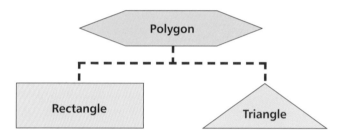

The virtue of inheritance is extremely powerful, and is the second principle of Object Oriented Programming (OOP).

A derived class declaration adds ( ) parentheses after its class name specifying the name of its parent base class.

Polygon.py

1 Create a new Python script that declares a base class with two class variables and a method to set their values

```
class Polygon :
        width = 0
        height = 0
        def set_values( self , width , height ) :
                Polygon.width = width
                Polygon.height = height
```

Rectangle.py

2 Next, create a script that declares a derived class with a method to return manipulated class variable values

```
from Polygon import *

class Rectangle( Polygon ) :
        def area( self ) :
                return self.width * self.height
```

3 Now, create another script that declares a derived class with a method to return manipulated class variable values

```
from Polygon import *

class Triangle( Polygon ) :
    def area( self ) :
        return ( self.width * self.height ) / 2
```

Triangle.py

4 Save the three class files then start a new Python script by making features of both derived classes available

```
from Rectangle import *
from Triangle import *
```

inherit.py

5 Next, create an instance of each derived class

```
rect = Rectangle()
trey = Triangle()
```

6 Now, call the class method inherited from the base class, passing arguments to assign to the class variables

```
rect.set_values( 4 , 5 )
trey.set_values( 4 , 5 )
```

Hot tip

A class declaration can derive from more than one class by listing multiple base classes in the parentheses after its name in the declaration.

7 Finally, display the result of manipulating the class variables inherited from the base class

```
print( 'Rectangle Area:' , rect.area() )
print( 'Triangle Area:' , trey.area() )
```

8 Save the file in your scripts directory, then open a Command Prompt window there and run this program – to see output get displayed using inherited features

```
C:\MyScripts>python inherit.py
Rectangle Area: 20
Triangle Area: 10.0

C:\MyScripts>
```

Beware

Don't confuse class instances and derived classes – an instance is a copy of a class, whereas a derived class is a new class that inherits properties of the base class from which it is derived.

127

Overriding base methods

A method can be declared in a derived class to override a matching method in the base class – if both method declarations have the same name and the same number of listed arguments. This effectively hides the base class method as it becomes inaccessible unless it is called explicitly, using the base class name for identification.

Where a method in a base class supplies a default argument value this can be used in an explicit call to the base method, or alternative values can be supplied by overriding methods.

Person.py

1 Create a new Python script that declares a base class with an initializer method to set an instance variable, and a second method to display that variable value
```
class Person :
```

```
    '''A base class to define Person properties.'''

    def __init__( self , name ) :
        self.name = name

    def speak( self , msg  = '(Calling The Base Class)' ) :
        print( self.name , msg )
```

Man.py

2 Next, create a script that declares a derived class with a method that overrides the second base class method
```
from Person import *
```

```
    '''A derived class to define Man properties.'''

class Man( Person ) :
    def speak( self , msg ) :
        print( self.name , ':\n\tHello!' , msg )
```

Hombre.py

3 Now, create another script that also declares a derived class with a method that once again overrides the same method in the base class
```
from Person import *
```

```
    '''A derived class to define Hombre properties.'''

class Hombre( Person ) :
    def speak( self , msg ) :
        print( self.name , ':\n\tHola!' , msg )
```

...cont'd

4 Save the three class files, then start a new Python script by making features of both derived classes available
from Man import *
from Hombre import *

override.py

5 Next, create an instance of each derived class, initializing the "name" instance variable attribute
guy_1 = Man('Richard')
guy_2 = Hombre('Ricardo')

6 Now, call the overriding methods of each derived class, assigning different values to the "msg" argument
guy_1.speak('It\'s a beautiful evening.\n')
guy_2.speak('Es una tarde hermosa.\n')

Man -Richard
    Hombre - Ricardo

129

7 Finally, explicitly call the base class method, passing a reference to each derived class – but none for the "msg" variable so its default value will be used
Person.speak(guy_1)
Person.speak(guy_2)

8 Save the file in your scripts directory, then open a Command Prompt window there and run this program – to see output from overriding and base class methods

```
C:\MyScripts>python override.py
Richard :
        Hello! It's a beautiful evening.

Ricardo :
        Hola! Es una tarde hermosa.

Richard (Calling The Base Class)
Ricardo (Calling The Base Class)

C:\MyScripts>
```

Don't forget

The method declaration in the derived class must exactly match that in the base class to override it.

Harnessing polymorphism

The three cornerstones of Object Oriented Programming (OOP) are encapsulation, inheritance, and polymorphism. Examples earlier in this chapter have demonstrated how data can be encapsulated within a Python class, and how derived classes inherit the properties of their base class. This example introduces the final cornerstone principle of polymorphism.

The term "polymorphism" (from Greek, meaning "many forms") describes the ability to assign a different meaning, or purpose, to an entity according to its context.

In Python, the + character entity can be described as polymorphic because it represents either the arithmetical addition operator, in the context of numerical operands, or the string concatenation operator, in the context of character operands.

Perhaps more importantly, Python class methods can also be polymorphic because the Python language uses "duck typing" – meaning... if it walks like a duck, swims like a duck, and quacks like a duck, then that bird is reckoned to be a duck.

In a duck-typed language you can create a function to take an object of any type and call that object's methods. If the object does indeed have the called methods (is reckoned to be a duck) they are executed, otherwise the function signals a run-time error.

Like-named methods of multiple classes can be created, and instances of those classes will execute the associated version.

Duck.py

1 Create a new Python script that declares a class with methods to display strings unique to the class

```python
class Duck :
        def talk( self ) :
                print( '\nDuck Says: Quack!' )
        def coat( self ) :
                print( 'Duck Wears: Feathers' )
```

Mouse.py

2 Next, create a Python script that declares a class with like-named methods, but to display strings unique to this class

```python
class Mouse :
        def talk( self ) :
                print( '\nMouse Says: Squeak!' )
        def coat( self ) :
                print( 'Mouse Wears: Fur' )
```

...cont'd

3 Save the two class files, then start a new Python script by making features of both classes available
```
from Duck import *
from Mouse import *
```

polymorph.py

4 Next, define a function that accepts any single object as its argument and attempts to call methods of that object
```
def describe( object ) :
        object.talk()
        object.coat()
```

Duck - donald

5 Now, create an instance object of each class
```
donald = Duck()
mickey = Mouse()
```

6 Finally, add statements to call the function and pass each instance object to it as an argument
```
describe( donald )
describe( mickey )
```

Mouse - mickey

131

7 Save the file in your scripts directory and open a Command Prompt window there, then run this program – to see the methods of associated versions get called

```
C:\MyScripts>python polymorph.py

Duck Says: Quack!
Duck Wears: Feathers

Mouse Says: Squeak!
Mouse Wears: Fur

C:\MyScripts>
```

Don't forget

A class can have only one method with a given name – method overloading is not supported in Python.

Object Oriented Programming with Python allows data encapsulation, inheritance, and polymorphism. Base class methods can be overridden by like-named methods in derived classes. Python does not, however, support the technique of "overloading" found in other languages – in which methods of the same name can be created with different argument lists in a single class.

Summary

- A class is a data structure prototype describing object properties with its methods and attribute members.

- Each class declaration begins with the **class** keyword, and is followed by an indented code block that may contain a class document string, class variables, and class methods.

- Class variables have global scope, but instance variables (declared within method definitions) have only local scope.

- Instance variables encapsulate data securely in a class structure, and are initialized when a class instance is created.

- Properties of a class are referenced by dot notation, and are addressed internally using the **self** prefix.

- A class instance is a copy of the prototype that automatically calls its **__init__()** method when the instance is first created.

- An attribute of a class can be added, modified, or removed using dot notation or manipulated using the built-in functions **getattr()**, **hasattr()**, **setattr()**, and **delattr()**.

- The name of attributes automatically supplied by Python begin with an underscore character to notionally indicate privacy.

- The built-in **__dict__** attribute contains a namespace dictionary of class component keys and values.

- Python automatically performs garbage collection, but the **del** keyword can remove objects and call the class destructor.

- A derived class inherits the method and attribute members of the parent base class from which it is derived.

- A method of a derived class can override a matching method of the same name in its parent base class.

- Python is a duck-typed language that supports polymorphism for like-named methods of multiple classes.

8 Processing requests

This chapter demonstrates how to create server-side Python scripts to process HTML web requests.

Sending responses

Whenever a user asks to view an online web page in their browser it requests the page from the web server, and receives the page in response, via the HTTP protocol.

Where a requested web page address is an HTML document (typically with an **.html** file extension), the web server response will return that file to the browser so its contents can be displayed.

The examples in this chapter use the free Abyss Personal Edition web server available at **www.aprelium.com**
Installed locally on your computer this can be addressed by the domain name **localhost** or by the IP address **127.0.0.1**.

Where Python is installed on the computer hosting the web server, the web server can be configured to recognize Python scripts (typically with a **.py** file extension) and call upon the Python interpreter to process script code before sending an HTML response to the web server, for return to the browser client.

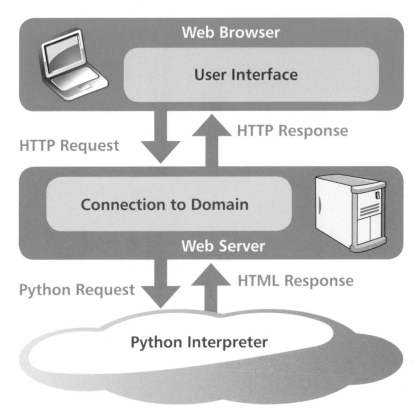

A Python script requested by a web browser can generate a complete HTML document response by describing the content type on the first line as **Content-type:text/html\r\n\r\n** so the web browser will parse the markup content for display on the screen.

1 Ensure the web server is running and configured to execute Python scripts

Interface	Interpreter	Associated Extensions		
CGI/ISAPI	C:\Python37\python.exe	py	✏️	🗑️
				Add

2 Next, start a new Python script by describing its generated output content type to be an HTML document

```
print( 'Content-type:text/html\r\n\r\n' )
```

response.py

3 Now, add statements to output an entire web page including all its HTML markup tags

```
print( '<!DOCTYPE HTML>' )
print( '<html lang="en">' )
print( '<head>' )
print( '<meta charset="UTF-8">' )
print( '<title>Python Response</title>' )
print( '</head>' )
print( '<body>' )
print( '<h1>Hello From Python Online!</h1>' )
print( '</body>' )
print( '</html>' )
```

The **Content-type** output description gets sent as an HTTP Header to the browser, and must appear on the first line.

4 Finally, save the file in the web server's HTML documents directory – typically this will be **/htdocs**

5 Open a web browser and request the script from the web server via the HTTP protocol – to see the HTML document response provided by the Python script

Enclose HTML attribute values within double quote marks so they do not get confused with the single quote marks enclosing the strings.

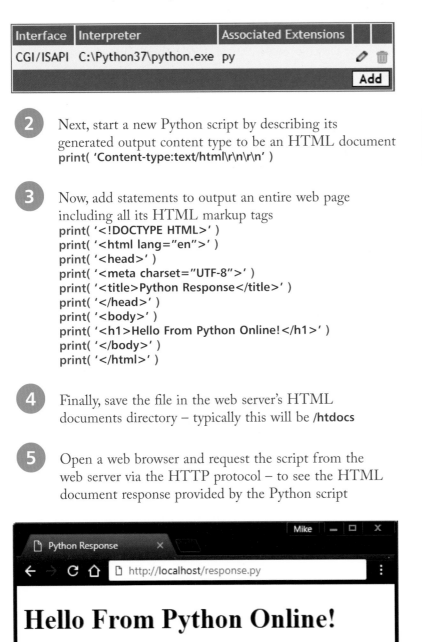

Mike

🗋 Python Response

← → C ⟳ 🗋 http://localhost/response.py

Hello From Python Online!

Handling values

Values can be passed to a Python script on the web server when the browser makes an HTTP request. Those values can be used in the script and echoed in a response returned to the browser.

Python's "cgi" module can be used to easily handle data passed from the web browser by an HTTP request. This provides a **FieldStorage()** constructor that creates an object storing the passed data as a dictionary of key:value pairs. Any individual value can then be retrieved by specifying its associated key name within the parentheses of that FieldStorage object's **getvalue()** method.

The browser can submit data to the script using a "GET" method that simply appends key=value pairs to the script's URL address. These follow a **?** question mark character after the file name and multiple pairs must be separated by an **&** ampersand character. For example, **script.py?key1=value1&key2=value2**.

get.html

 Create a new HTML document containing hyperlinks with appended values to pass to a Python script

```
<!DOCTYPE HTML>
<html lang="en">
<head>
<meta charset="UTF-8">
<title>Python Appended Values</title>
</head>
<body>
<h1>
<a href="get.py?make=Ferrari&model=Dino">Ferrari</a>
<a href="get.py?make=Fiat&model=Topolino">Fiat</a>
<a href="get.py?make=Ford&model=Mustang">Ford</a>
</h1>
</body>
</html>
```

get.py

2 Next, start a new Python script by making CGI handling features available and create a FieldStorage data object

```
import cgi

data = cgi.FieldStorage()
```

3 Now, assign two passed values to variables by specifying their associated key names

```
make = data.getvalue( 'make' )
model = data.getvalue( 'model' )
```

4 Then, add statements to output an entire HTML web page including passed values in the output

```
print( 'Content-type:text/html\r\n\r\n' )
print( '<!DOCTYPE HTML>' )
print( '<html lang="en">' )
print( '<head>' )
print( '<meta charset="UTF-8">' )
print( '<title>Python Response</title>' )
print( '</head>' )
print( '<body>' )
print( '<h1>' , make , model , '</h1>' )
print( '<a href="get.html">Back</a>' )
print( '</body>' )
print( '</html>' )
```

5 Finally, save both files in the web server's **/htdocs** directory

6 Open a web browser and load the HTML document, then click any hyperlink – to see passed values in the response

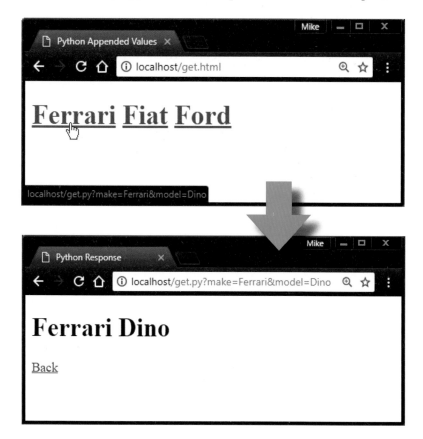

The request string in the GET method is limited to 1024 characters so is unsuitable for passing lots of key=value pairs.

The values appended to the URL are visible in the browser address field of the response, so the GET method should not be used to send passwords or other sensitive data values to the web server.

Submitting forms

Passing data from a web page to a web server using the GET method to append key:value pairs to a URL is simple, but has some limitations – the request string length cannot exceed 1024 characters, and the values appear in the browser address field.

As a more reliable alternative, the browser can submit data to the script using a "POST" method that sends the information to the web server as a separate message not appended to the URL.

Python's "cgi" module can be used to handle form data sent from the browser with the POST method in exactly the same way as data passed from the browser with the GET method. This module's **FieldStorage()** constructor can create an object to store the posted data as a dictionary of key:value pairs for each form field. Any individual value can be retrieved by specifying its associated key name to the object's **getvalue()** method.

post.html

post.py

1. Create a new HTML document containing a form with two text fields containing default values and a submit button to post all form values to a Python script

```
<!DOCTYPE HTML>
<html lang="en">
<head>
<meta charset="UTF-8">
<title>Python Form Values</title>
</head>
<body>
<form method="POST" action="post.py">
Make: <input type="text" name="make" value="Ford">
Model:
<input type="text" name="model" value="Mustang">
<p><input type="submit" value="Submit"></p>
</form>
</body>
</html>
```

2. Next, start a new Python script by making CGI handling features available and create a FieldStorage data object

```
import cgi
data = cgi.FieldStorage()
```

3. Now, assign two passed values to variables by specifying their associated key names

```
make = data.getvalue( 'make' )
model = data.getvalue( 'model' )
```

④ Then, add statements to output an entire HTML web page including posted values in the output

```
print( 'Content-type:text/html\r\n\r\n' )
print( '<!DOCTYPE HTML>' )
print( '<html lang="en">' )
print( '<head>' )
print( '<meta charset="UTF-8">' )
print( '<title>Python Response</title>' )
print( '</head>' )
print( '<body>' )
print( '<h1>' , make , model , '</h1>' )
print( '<a href="post.html">Back</a>' )
print( '</body>' )
print( '</html>' )
```

⑤ Finally, save both files in the web server's **/htdocs** directory

⑥ Open a web browser and load the HTML document, then push the button – to see posted values in the response

All the HTML documents in this chapter must be loaded into the browser via a web server domain such as **localhost** – you cannot simply open them directly to try these examples.

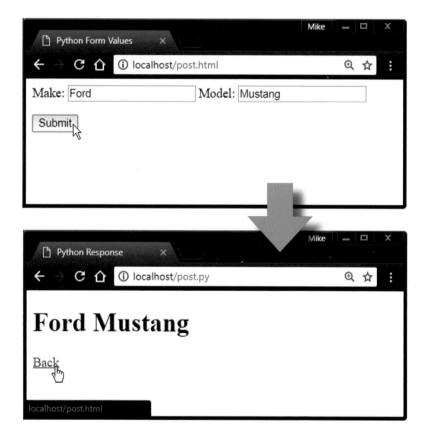

Click the Back hyperlink and change the text field values then submit the form again to see your new values echoed.

Providing text areas

Large amounts of user-input text data can be passed from a web page to a web server using HTML **<textarea>** tags and the form POST method. This tag has no **value** attribute so a default value may not be provided. It is, therefore, useful to have the Python script test whether the text area has been left blank and provide a default value when the user has entered no text.

text.html

1 Create a new HTML document containing a form with a text area field and a submit button

```
<!DOCTYPE HTML>
<html lang="en">
<head> <meta charset="UTF-8">
<title>Text Area Example</title> </head>
<body>
<form method="POST" action="text.py">
<textarea name="Future Web" rows="5" cols="40">
</textarea>
<input type="submit" value="Submit">
</form>
</body>
</html>
```

text.py

2 Next, start a new Python script by making CGI handling features available and create a FieldStorage data object

```
import cgi
data = cgi.FieldStorage()
```

3 Now, test if the text area is blank then assign its content string or a default string to a variable

```
if data.getvalue( 'Future Web' ) :
        text = data.getvalue( 'Future Web' )
else :
        text = 'Please Enter Text!'
```

4 Then, add statements to output an entire HTML web page including posted or default values in the output

```
print( 'Content-type:text/html\r\n\r\n' )
print( '<!DOCTYPE HTML>' )
print( '<html lang="en">' )
print( '<head> <meta charset="UTF-8">' )
print( '<title>Python Response</title> </head>' )
print( '<body>' )
print( '<h1>' , text , '</h1>' )
print( '<a href="text.html">Back</a>' )
print( '</body>' )
print( '</html>' )
```

5 Finally, save both files in the web server's **/htdocs** directory and load the HTML document in a browser, then push the form button – to see values in the response

Beware

The average character width may vary between browsers – so the physical size of the text area field may vary too.

6 Examine the HTTP request and response components using browser developer tools to see that the text gets sent as a separate message in the HTTP "Request body"

Hot tip

You can use the F12 Developer Tools in your web browser to examine the HTTP request and response components, as shown.

Checking boxes

An HTML form can provide a visual checkbox "on/off" switch that the user can toggle to include or exclude its associated data for submission to the web server. The Python script nominated to handle the form data can test whether each checkbox has been checked, simply by testing if a value has been received from the checkbox of that name.

check.html

1 Create a new HTML document containing a form with three checkboxes with associated values, and a submit button to post only checked values to a Python script

```
<!DOCTYPE HTML>
<html lang="en">
<head> <meta charset="UTF-8">
<title>Checkbox Example</title> </head>
<body>
<form method="POST" action="check.py">
Sailing:
<input type="checkbox" name="sail" value="Sailing">
Walking:
<input type="checkbox" name="walk" value="Walking">
Ski-ing:
<input type="checkbox" name="skee" value="Ski-ing">
</form>
</body>
</html>
```

check.py

2 Next, start a new Python script by making CGI handling features available and create a FieldStorage data object

```
import cgi
data = cgi.FieldStorage()
```

3 Now, assign a list of checked box values as elements of an unordered HTML list to a variable

```
list = '<ul>'

if data.getvalue( 'sail' ) :
        list += '<li>' + data.getvalue( 'sail' )

if data.getvalue( 'walk' ) :
        list += '<li>' + data.getvalue( 'walk' )

if data.getvalue( 'skee' ) :
        list += '<li>' + data.getvalue( 'skee' )

list += '</ul>'
```

4 Then, add statements to output an entire HTML web page including a list of posted values in the output

```
print( 'Content-type:text/html\r\n\r\n' )
print( '<!DOCTYPE HTML>' )
print( '<html lang="en">' )
print( '<head>' )
print( '<meta charset="UTF-8">' )
print( '<title>Python Response</title>' )
print( '</head>' )
print( '<body>' )
print( '<h1>' , list , '</h1>' )
print( '<a href="check.html">Back</a>' )
print( '</body>' )
print( '</html>' )
```

The **checked** keyword can be added in any checkbox **<input>** element to make it checked by default.

5 Finally, save both files in the web server's **/htdocs** directory and load the HTML document in a browser, then push the submit button – to see checked values in the response

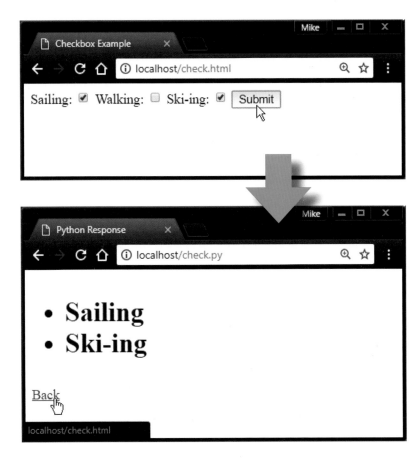

As the "Walking" checkbox is unchecked in this example, its key:value pair is not even sent to the web server.

Choosing radio buttons

An HTML form can provide a "radio button" group from which the user can select just one button to submit its associated data to the web server. Unlike checkboxes, radio buttons that share a common name are mutually exclusive, so when one button in the group is selected, all other buttons in that group are switched off. The Python script nominated to handle the form data can test the value submitted for the radio button group name and supply an appropriate response.

radio.html

 Create a new HTML document containing a form with one group of three radio buttons and a submit button to post the value of the chosen button to a Python script

```
<!DOCTYPE HTML>
<html lang="en">
<head> <meta charset="UTF-8">
<title>Radio Button Example</title> </head>
<body>
<form method="POST" action="radio.py">
<fieldset>
<legend>HTML Language Category?</legend>
Script
<input type="radio" name="cat" value="Script" checked>
Markup
<input type="radio" name="cat" value="Markup">
Program
<input type="radio" name="cat" value="Program">
<input type="submit" value="Submit">
</fieldset>
</form>
</body>
</html>
```

radio.py

2 Next, start a new Python script by making CGI handling features available and create a FieldStorage data object

```
import cgi
data = cgi.FieldStorage()
```

3 Now, test the submitted radio group value and assign an appropriate response to a variable

```
answer = data.getvalue( 'cat' )

if answer == 'Markup' :
        result = answer + ' Is Correct'
else :
        result = answer + ' Is Incorrect'
```

4 Then, add statements to output an entire HTML web page including the posted value in an appropriate output

```
print( 'Content-type:text/html\r\n\r\n' )
print( '<!DOCTYPE HTML>' )
print( '<html lang="en">' )
print( '<head>' )
print( '<meta charset="UTF-8">' )
print( '<title>Python Response</title>' )
print( '</head>' )
print( '<body>' )
print( '<h1>' , result , '</h1>' )
print( '<a href="radio.html">Back</a>' )
print( '</body>' )
print( '</html>' )
```

5 Finally, save both files in the web server's **/htdocs** directory

6 Load the HTML document in a browser, then choose the correct radio button answer and push the submit button – to see the associated chosen value in the response

Always include a **checked** attribute to automatically select one button in each radio button group – to include a default choice.

145

Radio button elements resemble the buttons on old radios where each button selected a particular radio station – but, of course, no two stations could be selected simultaneously.

Selecting options

An HTML form can provide a drop-down list of possible options from which the user can select a single option to include its associated data for submission to the web server. The submitted value can then be retrieved by specifying its associated list key name within the parentheses of that FieldStorage object's **getvalue()** method.

selection.html

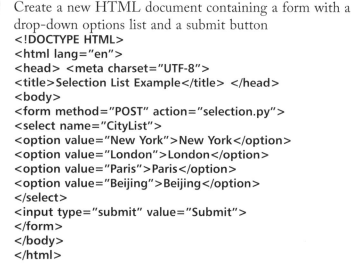

Create a new HTML document containing a form with a drop-down options list and a submit button

```
<!DOCTYPE HTML>
<html lang="en">
<head> <meta charset="UTF-8">
<title>Selection List Example</title> </head>
<body>
<form method="POST" action="selection.py">
<select name="CityList">
<option value="New York">New York</option>
<option value="London">London</option>
<option value="Paris">Paris</option>
<option value="Beijing">Beijing</option>
</select>
<input type="submit" value="Submit">
</form>
</body>
</html>
```

selection.py

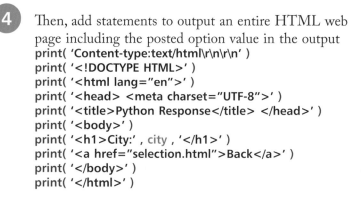

Next, start a new Python script by making CGI handling features available and create a FieldStorage data object

```
import cgi
data = cgi.FieldStorage()
```

Now, assign the selected option value to a variable

```
city = data.getvalue( 'CityList' )
```

Then, add statements to output an entire HTML web page including the posted option value in the output

```
print( 'Content-type:text/html\r\n\r\n' )
print( '<!DOCTYPE HTML>' )
print( '<html lang="en">' )
print( '<head> <meta charset="UTF-8">' )
print( '<title>Python Response</title> </head>' )
print( '<body>' )
print( '<h1>City:' , city , '</h1>' )
print( '<a href="selection.html">Back</a>' )
print( '</body>' )
print( '</html>' )
```

5 Finally, save both files in the web server's **/htdocs** directory and load the HTML document in a browser, then push the submit button – to see the selected value in the response

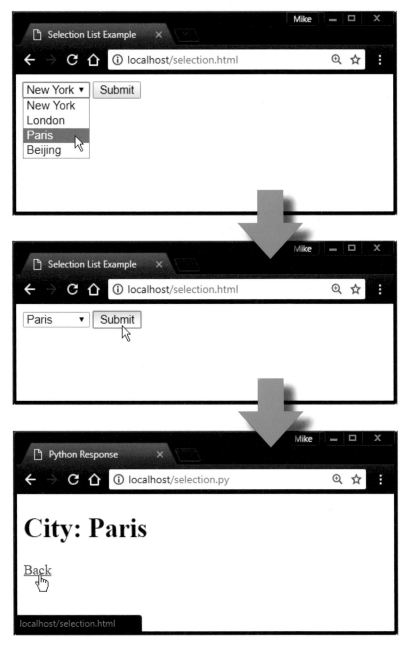

Typically, the first list option will be selected for submission by default, unless you click open the drop-down list and select an alternative.

You can include the **selected** attribute in an **<option>** tag to automatically select one option in each list – to include a default choice.

Uploading files

An HTML form can provide a file selection facility, which calls upon the operating system's "Choose File" dialog, to allow the user to browse their local file system and select a file. To enable this facility the HTML **<form>** tag must include an **enctype** attribute specifying the encoding type as "multipart/form-data".

The full path address of the file selected for upload is a value stored in the FieldStorage object list that can be accessed using its associated key name. Usefully, the file name can be stripped from the path address by the "os" module's **path.basename()** method.

A copy of an uploaded file can be written on the web server by reading from the FieldStorage object's **file** property.

upload.html

1 Create a new HTML document containing a form with a file selection facility and a submit button
```
<!DOCTYPE HTML>
<html lang="en">
<head> <meta charset="UTF-8">
<title>File Upload Example</title> </head>
<body>
<form method="POST" action="upload.py"
                    enctype="multipart/form-data" >
<input type="file" name="filename" style="width:400px">
<input type="submit" value="Submit">
</form>
</body>
</html>
```

upload.py

2 Next, start a new Python script by making CGI handling and operating system features available, then create a FieldStorage data object
```
import cgi , os
data = cgi.FieldStorage()
```

3 Now, assign the full path of the uploaded file to a variable and its stripped out file name to another variable
```
upload = data[ 'filename' ]
filename = os.path.basename( upload.filename )
```

4 Then, write a copy of the uploaded file on the web server
```
with open( filename , 'wb' ) as copy :
  copy.write( upload.file.read() )
```

...cont'd

5 Then, add statements to output an entire HTML web page including the uploaded file name in the output

```
print( 'Content-type:text/html\r\n\r\n' )
print( '<!DOCTYPE HTML>' )
print( '<html lang="en">' )
print( '<head>' )
print( '<meta charset="UTF-8">' )
print( '<title>Python Response</title>' )
print( '</head>' )
print( '<body>' )
print( '<h1>File Uploaded:' , filename , '</h1>' )
print( '<a href="upload.html">Back</a>' )
print( '</body>' )
print( '</html>' )
```

Notice that binary file mode is used here to copy the uploaded file.

6 Finally, save both files in the web server's **/htdocs** directory and load the HTML document in a browser, then select a file for upload – to see the file upload response

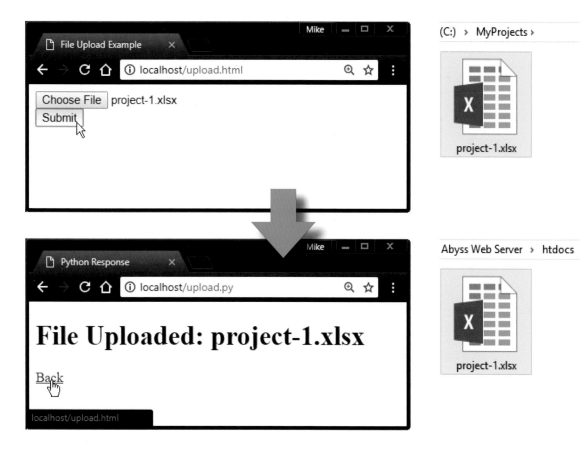

Summary

- Python can be installed on a web server host to process script code before sending a response to a web browser client.

- A server-side Python script can generate an HTML document by describing the content type as **Content-type:text/html\r\n\r\n**.

- The **cgi** module provides a **FieldStorage()** constructor to create an object for storing submitted data as key:value pairs.

- Any value stored in a FieldStorage object can be retrieved by specifying its key name to the object's **getvalue()** method.

- The browser can send data to a script using the GET method that appends key=value pairs to its URL address after a **?** mark.

- Multiple key=value pairs of data can be submitted using the GET method if each pair is separated by an **&** character.

- The GET method request string length cannot exceed 1024 characters and will be visible in the browser address field.

- The browser can send data to a script using the POST method that submits key=value pairs as a separate message.

- Data submitted from an HTML form can be stored in a FieldStorage object as key:value pairs for each form field.

- A server-side Python script can provide default values for submitted HTML form fields that the user has left blank.

- Checkbox fields of an HTML form that are unchecked do not get submitted to the web server.

- A selected radio button in a group provides the value to be associated with the group name when the form gets submitted.

- A selected item in a drop-down list provides the value to be associated with the list name when the form gets submitted.

- An HTML form can allow file uploads only if its **enctype** attribute specifies its encoding type as "multipart/form-data".

9 Building interfaces

This chapter demonstrates how to create graphical windowed applications with Python.

Launching a window

The standard Python module that you can use to create graphical applications is called "tkinter" – a <u>t</u>ool<u>k</u>it to <u>inter</u>face with the system GUI (Graphical User Interface).

The **tkinter** module can be imported into a program like any other module to provide attributes and methods for windowed apps. Every **tkinter** program must begin by calling the **Tk()** constructor to create a window object. The window's size can, optionally, be specified as a **'widthxheight'** string argument to the window object's **geometry()** method. Similarly, the window's title can be specified as a **'title'** string argument to the window object's **title()** method. If not specified, default size and title values will be used.

Every **tkinter** program must also call the window object's **mainloop()** method to capture events, such as when the user closes the window to quit the program. This loop should appear at the end of the program as it also handles window updates that may be implemented during execution.

With **tkinter**, all the graphical controls that can be included in the application window, such as buttons or checkboxes, are referred to as "widgets". Perhaps the simplest widget is a non-interactive label object that merely displays text or an image in the app interface. A label object can be created by specifying the window object's name and **text='string'** as arguments to a **Label()** constructor.

Once created, each widget, such as a label, must then be added to the window using one of these "geometry manager" methods:

- **pack()** – places the widget against a specified side of the window using **TOP**, **BOTTOM**, **LEFT**, or **RIGHT** constant values specified to its **side=** argument.

- **place()** – places the widget at XY coordinates in the window using numerical values specified to its **x=** and **y=** arguments.

- **grid()** – places the widget in a cell within the window using numerical values specified to its **row=** and **column=** arguments.

Optionally, the **pack()** method may include a **fill** argument to expand the widget in available space. For example, with **fill = 'x'**. Alternatively, the **pack()** method may include **padx** and **pady** arguments to expand the widget along an axis by a specified amount.

Beware

There can be only one call to the **Tk()** constructor and it must be at the start of the program code.

152

Hot tip

The **grid()** geometry manager method is demonstrated in the example on page 174.

1 Start a new Python script with a statement to make the "tkinter" module GUI methods and attributes available
from tkinter import *

2 Next, add a statement to call upon a constructor to create a window object
window = Tk()

3 Now, add a statement to specify a title for this window
window.title('Label Example')

4 Then, add a statement to call upon a constructor to create a label object
label = Label(window , text = 'Hello World!')

5 Use the packer to add the label to the window with both horizontal and vertical padding for positioning
label.pack(padx = 200 , pady = 50)

6 Finally, add the mandatory statement to maintain the window by capturing events
window.mainloop()

7 Save the program in your scripts directory, then open a Command Prompt window there and run this program with the command **python tk_window.py** – to see a window appear containing a label widget

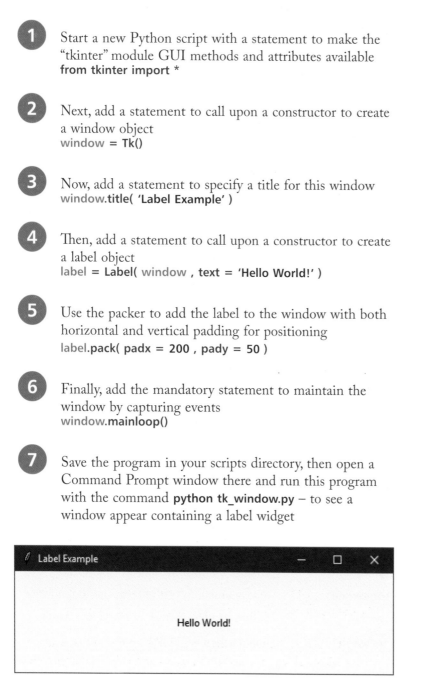

tk_window.py

153

Don't forget

Widgets will not appear in the window when running the program unless they have been added with a geometry manager.

Responding to buttons

A Button widget provides a graphical button in an application window that may contain either text or an image to convey the button's purpose. A button object is created by specifying the window name and options as arguments to a **Button()** constructor. Each option is specified as an option=value pair. The **command** option must always specify the name of a function or method to call when the user clicks that button. The most popular options are listed below, together with a brief description:

Option:	Description:
activebackground	Background color when the cursor is over
activeforeground	Foreground color when the cursor is over
bd	Border width in pixels (default is 2)
bg	Background color
command	Function to call when clicked
fg	Foreground color
font	Font for button label
height	Button height in text lines, or pixels for images
highlightcolor	Border color when in focus
image	Image to be displayed instead of text
justify	Multiple text lines as LEFT, CENTER, or RIGHT
padx	Horizontal padding
pady	Vertical padding
relief	Border style of SUNKEN, RIDGE, RAISED or GROOVE
state	Enabled status of NORMAL or DISABLED
underline	Index number in text of character to underline
width	Button width in letters, or pixels for images
wraplength	Length at which to wrap text

Hot tip

You can also call a button's **invoke()** method to, in turn, call the function nominated to its **command** option.

The values assigned to other options determine the widget's appearance. These can be altered by specifying a new option=value pair as an argument to the widget's **configure()** method. Additionally, a current option value can be retrieved by specifying its name as a string argument to the widget's **cget()** method.

1 Start a new Python script by making GUI features available then create a window and specify a title
```
from tkinter import *
window = Tk()
window.title( 'Button Example' )
```

tk_button.py

2 Next, create a button to exit the program when clicked
```
btn_end = Button( window , text = 'Close' , command=exit )
```

3 Now, add a function to toggle the window's background color when another button gets clicked
```
def tog() :
        if window.cget( 'bg' ) == 'yellow' :
                window.configure( bg = 'gray' )
        else :
                window.configure( bg = 'yellow' )
```

Beware

Only the function name is specified to the **command** option. Do not add trailing parentheses in the assignment.

4 Then, create a button to call the function when clicked
```
btn_tog = Button( window , text = 'Switch' , command=tog )
```

5 Add the buttons to the window with positional padding
```
btn_end.pack( padx = 150 , pady = 20 )
btn_tog.pack( padx = 150 , pady = 20 )
```

6 Finally, add the loop to capture this window's events
```
window.mainloop()
```

7 Save the file in your scripts directory, then open a Command Prompt window there and run this program with the command **python tk_button.py** – click the button to see the window's background color change

Hot tip

The 'gray' color is the original default color of the window.

Displaying messages

A program can display messages to the user by calling methods provided in the "tkinter.messagebox" module. This must be imported separately and its lengthy name can, usefully, be assigned a short alias by an **import as** statement.

A message box is created by supplying a box title and the message to be displayed as the two arguments to one of these methods:

Method:	Icon:	Buttons:
showinfo()	(i)	OK
showwarning()	⚠	OK
showerror()	✖	OK
askquestion()	(?)	Yes (returns the string 'yes') and No (returns the string 'no')
askokcancel()	(?)	OK (returns 1) and Cancel
askyesno()	(?)	Yes (returns 1) and No
askretrycancel()	(?)	Retry (returns 1) and Cancel

Hot tip

Only the **askquestion()** method returns two values – the **askyesno()** No button and both Cancel buttons return nothing.

Those methods that produce a message box containing a single OK button return no value when the button gets clicked by the user. Those that do return a value can be used to perform conditional branching by testing that value.

1 Start a new Python program by making GUI features available and messagebox features available as a short alias
from tkinter import *
import tkinter.messagebox as box

tk_message.py

2 Next, create a window object and specify a title
window = Tk()
window.title('Message Box Example')

3 Add a function to display various message boxes
```
def dialog() :
        var = box.askyesno( 'Message Box' , 'Proceed?' )
        if var == 1 :
                box.showinfo( 'Yes Box', 'Proceeding...' )
        else :
                box.showwarning( 'No Box', 'Canceling...' )
```

4 Then, create a button to call the function when clicked
btn = Button(window , text = 'Click' , command=dialog)

5 Add the button to the window with positional padding
btn.pack(padx = 150 , pady = 50)

6 Finally, add the loop to capture this window's events
window.mainloop()

7 Save the file in your scripts directory, then open a Command Prompt window there and run this program with the command **python tk_message.py** – click the button to see the message boxes appear

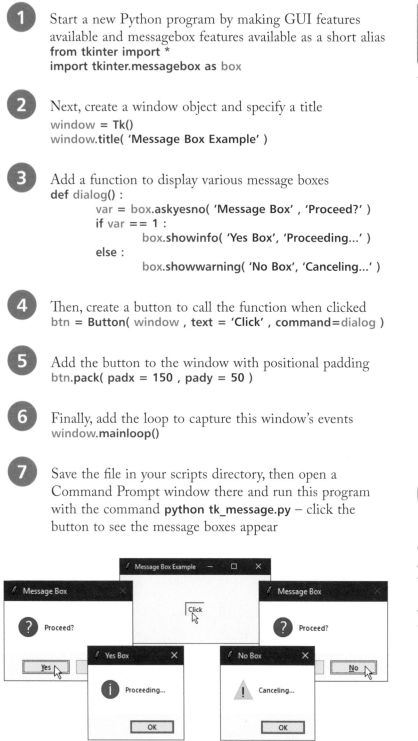

Options can be added as a third argument to these method calls. For example, add **type='abortretryignore'** to get three buttons.

Gathering entries

An Entry widget provides a single-line input field in an application where the program can gather entries from the user. An entry object is created by specifying the name of its parent container, such as a window or frame name, and options as arguments to an **Entry()** constructor. Each option is specified as an option=value pair. Popular options are listed below, together with a brief description:

Option:	Description:
bd	Border width in pixels (default is 2)
bg	Background color
fg	Foreground color used to render the text
font	Font for the text
highlightcolor	Border color when in focus
selectbackground	Background color of selected text
selectforeground	Foreground color of selected text
show	Hide password characters with show='*'
state	Enabled status of NORMAL or DISABLED
width	Entry width in letters

Multiple widgets can be grouped in frames for better positioning. A frame object is created by specifying the name of the window to a **Frame()** constructor. The frame's name can then be specified as the first argument to the widget constructors to identify it as that widget's container.

When actually adding widgets to the frame you can specify which side to pack them to in the frame with **TOP, BOTTOM, LEFT,** or **RIGHT** constants. For example, **entry.pack(side=LEFT)**.

Typically, an entry widget will appear alongside a label describing the type of input expected there from the user, or alongside a button widget that the user can click to perform some action on the data they have entered, so positioning in a frame is ideal.

Data currently entered into an entry widget can be retrieved by the program using that widget's **get()** method.

Hot tip

Use the Text widget instead of an Entry widget if you want to allow the user to enter multiple lines of text.

① Start a new Python program by making GUI features available and messagebox features available as a short alias
```
from tkinter import *
import tkinter.messagebox as box
```

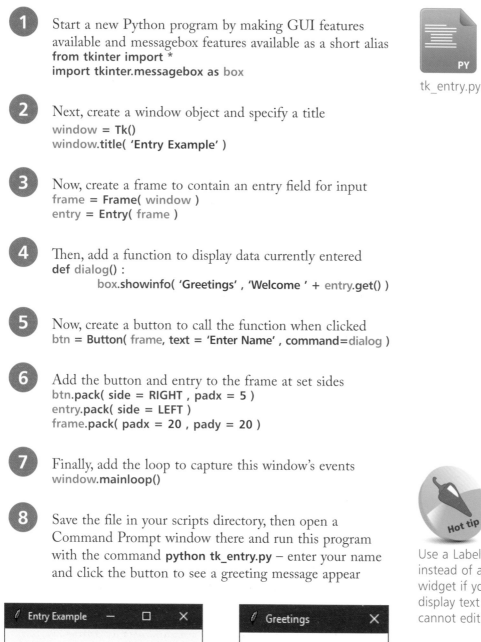
tk_entry.py

② Next, create a window object and specify a title
```
window = Tk()
window.title( 'Entry Example' )
```

③ Now, create a frame to contain an entry field for input
```
frame = Frame( window )
entry = Entry( frame )
```

④ Then, add a function to display data currently entered
```
def dialog() :
        box.showinfo( 'Greetings' , 'Welcome ' + entry.get() )
```

⑤ Now, create a button to call the function when clicked
```
btn = Button( frame, text = 'Enter Name' , command=dialog )
```

⑥ Add the button and entry to the frame at set sides
```
btn.pack( side = RIGHT , padx = 5 )
entry.pack( side = LEFT )
frame.pack( padx = 20 , pady = 20 )
```

⑦ Finally, add the loop to capture this window's events
```
window.mainloop()
```

⑧ Save the file in your scripts directory, then open a Command Prompt window there and run this program with the command **python tk_entry.py** – enter your name and click the button to see a greeting message appear

Hot tip

Use a Label widget instead of an Entry widget if you want to display text that the user cannot edit.

Listing options

A Listbox widget provides a list of items in an application from which the user can make a selection. A listbox object is created by specifying the name of its parent container, such as a window or frame name, and options as arguments to a **Listbox()** constructor. Popular options are listed below, together with a brief description:

Option:	Description:
bd	Border width in pixels (default is 2)
bg	Background color
fg	Foreground color used to render the text
font	Font for the text
height	Number of lines in list (default is 10)
selectbackground	Background color of selected text
selectmode	SINGLE (the default) or MULTIPLE selections
width	Listbox width in letters (default is 20)
yscrollcommand	Attach to a vertical scrollbar

With Tkinter, a scrollbar is a separate widget that can be attached to Listbox, Text, Canvas and Entry widgets.

Items are added to the listbox by specifying a list index number and the item string as arguments to its **insert()** method.

You can retrieve any item from a listbox by specifying its index number within the parentheses of its **get()** method. Usefully, a listbox also has a **curselection()** method that returns the index number of the currently-selected item, so this can be supplied as the argument to its **get()** method to retrieve the current selection.

tk_listbox.py

1 Start a new Python program by making GUI features available and messagebox features available as a short alias
from tkinter import *
import tkinter.messagebox as box

2 Next, create a window object and specify a title
window = **Tk()**
window.**title(** 'Listbox Example' **)**

3 Now, create a frame to contain widgets
frame = **Frame(** window **)**

4 Create a listbox widget offering three list items
```
listbox = Listbox( frame )
listbox.insert( 1 , 'HTML5 in easy steps' )
listbox.insert( 2 , 'CSS3 in easy steps' )
listbox.insert( 3 , 'JavaScript in easy steps' )
```

5 Next, add a function to display a listbox selection
```
def dialog() :
        box.showinfo( 'Selection' , 'Your Choice: ' + \
        listbox.get( listbox.curselection() ) )
```

6 Now, create a button to call the function when clicked
```
btn = Button( frame , text = 'Choose' , command = dialog )
```

7 Then, add the button and listbox to the frame at set sides
```
btn.pack( side = RIGHT , padx = 5 )
listbox.pack( side = LEFT )
frame.pack( padx = 30 , pady = 30 )
```

8 Finally, add the loop to capture this window's events
```
window.mainloop()
```

9 Save the file in your scripts directory, then open a Command Prompt window there and run this program with the command **python tk_listbox.py** – select an option and click the button to see your selection confirmed

If the **selectmode** is set to MULTIPLE, the **curselection()** method returns a tuple of the selected index numbers.

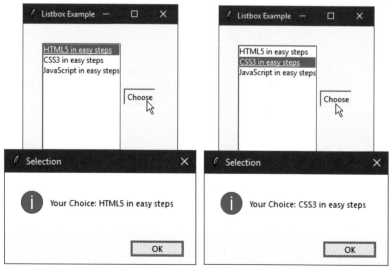

Polling radio buttons

A Radiobutton widget provides a single item in an application that the user may select. Where a number of radio buttons are grouped together, the user may only select any one item in the group. With tkinter, radio button objects are grouped together when they nominate the same control variable object to assign a value to upon selection. An empty string variable object can be created for this purpose using the **StringVar()** constructor or an empty integer variable object using the **IntVar()** constructor.

A radio button object is created by specifying four arguments to a **Radiobutton()** constructor:

● Name of the parent container, such as the frame name.

● Text for a display label, specified as a **text**=text pair.

● Control variable object, specified as a **variable**=variable pair.

● Value to be assigned, specified as a **value**=value pair.

Each radio button object has a **select()** method that can be used to specify a default selection in a group of radio buttons when the program starts. A string value assigned by selecting a radio button can be retrieved from a string variable object by its **get()** method.

Beware

You cannot use a regular variable to store values assigned from a radio button selection – it must be an object.

tk_radio.py

 Start a new Python program by making GUI features available and messagebox features available as a short alias
from tkinter import *
import tkinter.messagebox as box

 Next, create a window object and specify a title
window = Tk()
window.title('Radio Button Example')

 Now, create a frame to contain widgets
frame = Frame(window)

4 Then, construct a string variable object to store a selection
book = StringVar()

5 Next, create three radio button widgets whose value will be assigned to the string variable upon selection

```
radio_1 = Radiobutton( frame , text = 'HTML5' , \
        variable = book , value = 'HTML5 in easy steps' )
radio_2 = Radiobutton( frame , text = 'CSS3' , \
        variable = book , value = 'CSS3 in easy steps' )
radio_3 = Radiobutton( frame , text = 'JS' , \
        variable = book , value = 'JavaScript in easy steps' )
```

6 Now, add a statement to specify which radio button will be selected by default when the program starts

```
radio_1.select()
```

7 Then, add a function to display a radio button selection and a button to call this function

```
def dialog() :
        box.showinfo( 'Selection' , \
        'Your Choice: \n' + book.get() )
btn = Button( frame , text = 'Choose' , command = dialog )
```

8 Add the push button and radio buttons to the frame

```
btn.pack( side = RIGHT , padx = 5 )
radio_1.pack( side = LEFT )
radio_2.pack( side = LEFT )
radio_3.pack( side = LEFT )
frame.pack( padx = 30 , pady = 30 )
```

9 Finally, add the loop to capture this window's events

```
window.mainloop()
```

10 Save the file in your scripts directory, then open a Command Prompt window there and run this program with the command **python tk_radio.py** – choose an option and click the button to see your choice confirmed

A Radiobutton object has a **deselect()** method that can be used to cancel a selection programmatically.

163

Checking boxes

A Checkbutton widget provides a single item in an application that the user may select. Where a number of check buttons appear together the user may select one or more items. Check button objects nominate an individual control variable object to assign a value to whether checked or unchecked. An empty string variable object can be created for this using the **StringVar()** constructor or an empty integer variable object using the **IntVar()** constructor.

A check button object is created by specifying five arguments to a **Checkbutton()** constructor:

● Name of the parent container, such as the frame name.

● Text for a display label, as a **text=**text pair.

● Control variable object, as a **variable=**variable pair.

● Value to assign if checked, as an **onvalue=**value pair.

● Value to assign if unchecked, as an **offvalue=**value pair.

An integer value assigned by a check button can be retrieved from a integer variable object by its **get()** method.

tk_check.py

 Start a new Python program by making GUI features available and messagebox features available as a short alias
from tkinter import *
import tkinter.messagebox as box

 Next, create a window object and specify a title
window = Tk()
window.title('Check Button Example')

 Now, create a frame to contain widgets
frame = Frame(window)

4 Then, construct three integer variable objects to store values
var_1 = IntVar()
var_2 = IntVar()
var_3 = IntVar()

5 Create three check button widgets whose values will be assigned to the integer variable whether checked or not

```
book_1 = Checkbutton( frame , text = 'HTML5' , \
        variable = var_1 , onvalue = 1 , offvalue = 0 )
book_2 = Checkbutton( frame , text = 'CSS3' , \
        variable = var_2 , onvalue = 1 , offvalue = 0 )
book_3 = Checkbutton( frame , text = 'JS' , \
        variable = var_3 , onvalue = 1 , offvalue = 0 )
```

6 Next, add a function to display a check button selection

```
def dialog() :
        str = 'Your Choice:'
        if var_1.get() == 1 : str += '\nHTML5 in easy steps'
        if var_2.get() == 1 : str += '\nCSS3 in easy steps'
        if var_3.get() == 1 : str += '\nJavaScript in easy steps'
        box.showinfo( 'Selection' , str )
```

7 Now, create a button to call the function when clicked

```
btn = Button( frame , text = 'Choose' , command = dialog )
```

8 Then, add the push button and check buttons to the frame

```
btn.pack( side = RIGHT , padx = 5 )
book_1.pack( side = LEFT )
book_2.pack( side = LEFT )
book_3.pack( side = LEFT )
frame.pack( padx = 30, pady = 30 )
```

9 Finally, add the loop to capture this window's events

```
window.mainloop()
```

10 Save the file in your scripts directory, then open a Command Prompt window there and run this program with the command **python tk_check.py** – check some boxes and click the button to see your selection confirmed

A Checkbutton object has **select()** and **deselect()** methods that can be used to turn the state on or off. For example, **check_1.select()**.

The state of any Checkbutton object can be reversed by calling its **toggle()** method.

165

Adding images

With the **tkinter** module, images in GIF or PGM/PPM file formats can be displayed on Label, Button, Text and Canvas widgets using the **PhotoImage()** constructor to create image objects. This simply requires a single **file=** argument to specify the image file. Interestingly, it also has a **subsample()** method that can scale down a specified image by stating a sample value to **x=** and **y=** arguments. For example, values of **x=2**, **y=2** samples every second pixel – so the image object is half-size of the original.

Once an image object has been created, it can be added to a Label or Button constructor statement by an **image=** option.

Text objects have an **image_create()** method with which to embed an image into the text field. This requires two arguments to specify location and **image=**. For example, '**1.0**' specifies the first line and first character.

Canvas objects have a **create_image()** method that requires two arguments to specify location and **image=**. Here, the location sets the x,y coordinates on the canvas at which to paint the image.

The PhotoImage class also has a **zoom()** method that will double the image size with the same **x=2,y=2** values.

tk_image.py

python.gif
(200 x 200)

1 Start a new Python program by making GUI methods and attributes available, then create a window object and specify a title
```
from tkinter import *
window = Tk()
window.title( 'Image Example' )
```

2 Now, create an image object from a local image file
```
img = PhotoImage( file = 'python.gif' )
```

3 Then, create a label object to display the image above a colored background
```
label = Label( window , image = img , bg = 'yellow' )
```

4 Create a half-size image object from the first image object
```
small_img = PhotoImage.subsample( img , x = 2 , y = 2 )
```

5 Now, create a button to display the small image
```
btn = Button( window , image = small_img )
```

6 Create a text field and embed the small image, then insert some text after it

```
txt = Text( window , width = 25 , height = 7 )
txt.image_create( '1.0' , image = small_img )
txt.insert( '1.1', 'Python Fun!' )
```

7 Create a canvas and paint the small image above a colored background, then paint a diagonal line over the top of it

```
can = \
Canvas( window , width = 100 , height = 100 , bg = 'cyan' )
can.create_image( ( 50 , 50 ), image = small_img )
can.create_line( 0 , 0 , 100 , 100, width = 25 , fill = 'yellow' )
```

8 Then, add the widgets to the window

```
label.pack( side = TOP )
btn.pack( side = LEFT , padx = 10 )
txt.pack( side = LEFT )
can.pack( side = LEFT, padx = 10 )
```

9 Finally, add the loop to capture this window's events

```
window.mainloop()
```

10 Save the file in your scripts directory, then open a Command Prompt window there and run this program with the command **python tk_image.py** – to see the image

Notice that the Text method is **image_create()** but the Canvas method is **create_image()** – similar yet different.

Text and Canvas widgets are both powerful and flexible – discover more at **docs.python.org/3.7/library/tkinter.html**

Summary

- The **tkinter** module can be imported into a Python program to provide attributes and methods for windowed applications.

- Every **tkinter** program must begin by calling **Tk()** to create a window and call its **mainloop()** method to capture events.

- The window object's title is specified by its **title()** method.

- A label widget is created by specifying the name of its parent container and its text as arguments to the **Label()** constructor.

- Widgets can be added to an application using the **pack()**, **grid()** or **place()** geometry managers.

- A button widget is created by specifying the name of its parent container, its text, and the name of a function to call when the user pushes it, as arguments to the **Button()** constructor.

- The **tkinter.messagebox** module can be imported into a Python program to provide attributes and methods for message boxes.

- Message boxes that ask the user to make a choice return a value to the program for conditional branching.

- The **Frame()** constructor creates a container in which multiple widgets can be grouped for better positioning.

- The **Entry()** constructor creates a single line text field whose current contents can be retrieved by its **get()** method.

- Items are added to a **Listbox** object by its **insert()** method, and retrieved by specifying their index number to its **get()** method.

- **Radiobutton** and **Checkbutton** objects store values in the **StringVar** or **IntVar** object nominated by their **variable** attribute.

- The **PhotoImage()** constructor creates an image object that has a **subsample()** method that can scale down the image.

- Images can be added to **Button** and **Label** objects, embedded in **Text** objects, and painted on **Canvas** objects.

10

Developing applications

This chapter brings together elements from previous chapters to build a complete Python application.

Generating random numbers

The graphical application developed on subsequent pages of this book will generate six random numbers within a specific range. Initially, its functionality can be developed as a console application then transferred later to illustrate how it can be applied to graphical widget components.

The standard Python library has a **random** module that provides methods to generate pseudo-random numbers. The current system time is used by default to "seed" the random generator whenever it gets initialized – so it does not repeat its selections.

A pseudo-random floating-point number from 0.0 to 1.0 can be generated by calling the **random()** method from the **random** module. The range of generated numbers can be modified using the * multiplication operator to specify a maximum value, and can be rounded down to integer values using the built-in **int()** function. For example, to generate an integer within the range of zero to nine:

int(random.random() * 10)

Or to generate a whole number within the range of one to 10:

int(random.random() * 10) + 1

This statement could be used in a loop to generate multiple random integers within a given range, but any number may be repeated in that output – there is no guaranteed uniqueness. Instead, multiple unique random integers within a given range can be generated by the **sample()** method from the **random** module. This requires two arguments to specify the range and the number of unique integers to be returned. It is convenient to use the built-in **range()** function to specify a maximum value. For example, to generate six unique numbers within the range of zero to nine:

random.sample(range(10) , 6)

Or to generate six unique numbers within the range of one to ten:

random.sample(range(1 , 11) , 6)

This technique could represent a random lottery entry by choosing, say, six unique numbers between one and 59.

Beware

Floating-point numbers cast from the **float** data type to the **int** data type by the built-in **int()** function get truncated at the decimal point.

Don't forget

The **range()** function can specify start and end values. If no starting value is supplied, zero is assumed by default.

1 Launch a plain text editor, then begin a Python program by importing two functions from the "random" module
from random import random , sample

sample.py

2 Next, assign a random floating-point number to a variable, then display its value
num = random()
print('Random Float 0.0-1.0 : ' , num)

3 Now, multiply the floating-point number and cast it to become an integer then display its value
num = int(num * 10)
print('Random Integer 0 - 9 : ' , num)

4 Add a loop to assign multiple random integers to a list then display the list items
nums = [] ; i = 0
while i < 6 :
        nums.append(int(random() * 10) + 1)
        i += 1
print('Random Multiple Integers 1-10 :' , nums)

5 Finally, assign multiple unique random integers to the list then display the list items
nums = sample(range(1, 59) , 6)
print('Random Integer Sample 1 - 59 : ' , nums)

6 Save the file, then execute the program several times – to see the generated random numbers

Hot tip

The **random.sample()** function returns a list but does not actually replace any elements in the specified range.

```
Command Prompt                                    —    □    ×

C:\MyScripts>python sample.py
Random Float 0.0-1.0 :   0.6661321592513995
Random Integer 0 - 9 :   6
Random Multiple Integers 1-10:   [8, 4, 7, 8, 6, 5]
Random Integer Sample 1 - 59 :   [57, 34, 50, 48, 58, 2]

C:\MyScripts>python sample.py
Random Float 0.0-1.0 :   0.42563236001127547
Random Integer 0 - 9 :   4
Random Multiple Integers 1-10:   [6, 7, 3, 7, 1, 1]
Random Integer Sample 1 - 59 :   [23, 36, 47, 56, 2, 42]

C:\MyScripts>
```

Planning the program

When creating a new graphical application it is useful to first spend some time planning its design. Clearly define the program's precise purpose, decide what application functionality will be required, then decide what interface widgets will be needed.

A plan for a simple application to pick numbers for a lottery entry might look like this:

Program purpose

● The program will generate a series of six unique random numbers in the range 1-59 and have the ability to be reset.

Functionality required

● A function to generate and display six unique random numbers.

● A function to clear the last six random numbers from display.

Interface widgets needed

● One non-resizable window to contain all other widgets and to display the application title.

● One Label widget to display a static application logo image – just to enhance the appearance of the interface.

● Six Label widgets to dynamically display the generated series of unique random numbers – one number per Label.

● One Button widget to generate and display the numbers in the Label widgets when this Button gets clicked. This Button will not be enabled when the numbers <u>are</u> on display.

● One Button widget to clear the numbers on display in the Label widgets when this Button gets clicked. This Button will not be enabled when the numbers <u>are not</u> on display.

Having established a program plan means you can now produce the application basics by creating all the necessary widgets.

Hot tip

Toggle the value of a **Button** widget's **state** property from **NORMAL** to **DISABLED** to steer the user – in this case the application must be reset before a further series of unique random numbers can be generated.

1 Launch a plain text editor, then begin a Python program by importing all features from the "tkinter" module
```
# Widgets:
from tkinter import *
```

lotto(widgets).py

lotto.gif

2 Next, add statements to create a window object and an image object
```
window = Tk()
img = PhotoImage( file = 'logo.gif' )
```

3 Now, add statements to create all the necessary widgets
```
imgLbl = Label( window, image = img )
label1 = Label( window, relief = 'groove', width = 2 )
label2 = Label( window, relief = 'groove', width = 2 )
label3 = Label( window, relief = 'groove', width = 2 )
label4 = Label( window, relief = 'groove', width = 2 )
label5 = Label( window, relief = 'groove', width = 2 )
label6 = Label( window, relief = 'groove', width = 2 )
getBtn = Button( window )
resBtn = Button( window )
```

Don't forget

The **relief** property specifies a border style, and the **width** property specifies the label width in character numbers.

4 Then, add the widgets to the window using the grid layout manager – ready to receive arguments to specify how the widgets should be positioned at the design stage next
```
# Geometry:
imgLbl.grid()
label1.grid()
label2.grid()
label3.grid()
label4.grid()
label5.grid()
label6.grid()
getBtn.grid()
resBtn.grid()
```

5 Finally, add a loop statement to sustain the window
```
# Sustain window:
window.mainloop()
```

6 Save the file, then execute the program – to see the window appear containing all the necessary widgets

Designing the interface

Having created all the necessary widgets on the previous page, you can now design the interface layout by adding arguments to specify how the widgets should be positioned. A horizontal design will position the logo Label on the left, and on its right all six other Labels in a row with both Buttons below this. The grid layout manager, which positions widgets in rows and columns, can easily produce this design by allowing the logo Label to span a row containing all six other Labels and also a row containing both Buttons. One Button can span four columns and the other Button can span two columns, arranged like this:

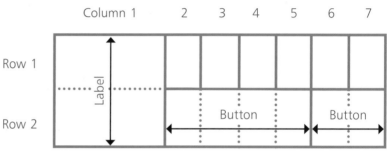

lotto(layout).py

Hot tip

The grid layout manager's **rowspan** and **columnspan** properties work like the HTML **rowspan** and **colspan** table cell attributes.

1 Edit the program started on the page 173 – firstly by positioning the Label containing the logo in the first column of the first row, and have it span across the second row
```
# Geometry:
imgLbl.grid( row = 1, column = 1, rowspan = 2 )
```

2 Next, position a Label in the second column of the first row, and add 10 pixels of padding to its left and right
```
label1.grid( row = 1, column = 2, padx = 10 )
```

3 Now, position a Label in the third column of the first row, and add 10 pixels of padding to its left and right
```
label2.grid( row = 1, column = 3, padx = 10 )
```

4 Position a Label in the fourth column of the first row, and add 10 pixels of padding to its left and right
```
label3.grid( row = 1, column = 4, padx = 10 )
```

5 Position a Label in the fifth column of the first row, and add 10 pixels of padding to its left and right
`label4.grid( row = 1, column = 5, padx = 10 )`

6 Position a Label in the sixth column of the first row, and add 10 pixels of padding to its left and right
`label5.grid( row = 1, column = 6, padx = 10 )`

7 Position a Label in the seventh column of the first row, then add 10 pixels of padding to the left side of the Label and 20 pixels of padding to the right side of the Label
`label6.grid( row = 1, column = 7, padx = ( 10, 20 ) )`

8 Next, position a Button in the second column of the second row, and have it span across four columns
`getBtn.grid( row = 2, column = 2, columnspan = 4 )`

9 Now, position a Button in the sixth column of the second row, and have it span across two columns
`resBtn.grid( row = 2, column = 6, columnspan = 2 )`

10 Save the file, then execute the program – to see the window appear containing all the necessary widgets now arranged in your grid layout design

Additional padding to the right of the Label in the final column of the first row extends the window width to simply create a small right-hand margin area.

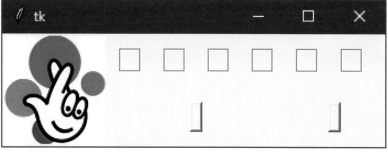

The Buttons will expand to fit static text that will appear on each Button face – specified in the next stage.

The window size is automatically adjusted to suit the grid contents, and the Button widgets are automatically centered in the spanned column width.

Assigning static properties

Having arranged all the necessary widgets in a grid layout on pages 174-175, you can now assign static values to the widgets. These values <u>will not</u> change during execution of the program.

lotto(static).py

1 Modify the program on pages 174-175 by inserting a new section just before the final loop statement, which begins with a statement specifying a window title
 # Static Properties:
window.title('Lotto Number Picker')

2 Next, add a statement to prevent the user resizing the window along both the X axis and the Y axis – this will disable the window's "resize" button
window.resizable(0, 0)

3 Now, add a statement to specify text to appear on the face of the first Button widget
getBtn.configure(text = 'Get My Lucky Numbers')

4 Then, add a statement to specify text to appear on the face of the second Button widget
resBtn.configure(text = 'Reset')

5 Save the file, then execute the program – to see the window now has a title, its resize button is disabled, and the buttons have now been resized to suit their text

The widget's **configure()** method allows properties to be subsequently added or modified after they have been created.

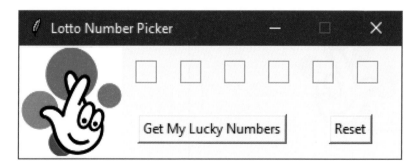

Initializing dynamic properties

Having specified values for static properties on the facing page, initial values can now be specified for those properties whose values <u>will</u> change dynamically during execution of the program.

 1 Modify the program on the facing page by inserting another new section just before the final loop statement, which specifies that each small empty Label should initially display an ellipsis

```
# Initial Properties:
label1.configure( text = '...' )

label2.configure( text = '...' )

label3.configure( text = '...' )

label4.configure( text = '...' )

label5.configure( text = '...' )

label6.configure( text = '...' )
```

lotto(initial).py

2 Next, add a statement to specify that the second Button widget should initially be disabled

```
resBtn.configure( state = DISABLED )
```

3 Save the file, then execute the program – to see each small Label now displays an ellipsis and that the "Reset" Button has been disabled

Lotto Number Picker — □ ✕

... ...

Get My Lucky Numbers   Reset

Don't forget

Button states are recognized by **tkinter** constants of **DISABLED** (off), **NORMAL** (on), or **ACTIVE** (pressed).

Adding runtime functionality

Having created code to initialize dynamic properties on pages 176-177, you can now add runtime functionality to respond to clicks on the Button widgets during execution of the program.

lotto.py

 Modify the program on pages 176-177 by inserting one more new section just before the final loop statement, which begins by making the **sample()** function available from the "random" module

```
# Dynamic Properties:
from random import sample
```

 Next, define a function that generates and assigns six unique random numbers to the small Labels and reverses the state of both Buttons

```
def pick() :
        nums = sample( range( 1, 59 ), 6 )
        label1.configure( text = nums[0] )
        label2.configure( text = nums[1] )
        label3.configure( text = nums[2] )
        label4.configure( text = nums[3] )
        label5.configure( text = nums[4] )
        label6.configure( text = nums[5] )
        getBtn.configure( state = DISABLED )
        resBtn.configure( state = NORMAL )
```

 Now, define a function to display an ellipsis on each small Label and revert both Buttons to their initial states

```
def reset() :
        label1.configure( text = '...' )
        label2.configure( text = '...' )
        label3.configure( text = '...' )
        label4.configure( text = '...' )
        label5.configure( text = '...' )
        label6.configure( text = '...' )
        getBtn.configure( state = NORMAL )
        resBtn.configure( state = DISABLED )
```

Hot tip

These steps provide comparable functionality to that of the console application on page 171.

 Then, add statements to nominate the relevant function to be called when each Button is pressed by the user

```
getBtn.configure( command = pick )
resBtn.configure( command = reset )
```

5 Finally, save the file – the complete program should look like that shown opposite

178

```
lotto.py - C:\MyScripts\lotto.py                                    —    □    ×
File  Edit  Format  Run  Options  Window  Help
# Widgets:
from tkinter import *
window = Tk()
img = PhotoImage( file = 'logo.gif' )
imgLbl = Label( window, image = img )
label1 = Label( window, relief = 'groove', width = 2 )
label2 = Label( window, relief = 'groove', width = 2 )
label3 = Label( window, relief = 'groove', width = 2 )
label4 = Label( window, relief = 'groove', width = 2 )
label5 = Label( window, relief = 'groove', width = 2 )
label6 = Label( window, relief = 'groove', width = 2 )
getBtn = Button( window )
resBtn = Button( window )

# Geometry:
imgLbl.grid( row = 1, column = 1, rowspan = 2 )
label1.grid( row = 1, column = 2, padx = 10 )
label2.grid( row = 1, column = 3, padx = 10 )
label3.grid( row = 1, column = 4, padx = 10 )
label4.grid( row = 1, column = 5, padx = 10 )
label5.grid( row = 1, column = 6, padx = 10 )
label6.grid( row = 1, column = 7, padx = ( 10, 20 ) )
getBtn.grid( row = 2, column = 2, columnspan = 4 )
resBtn.grid( row = 2, column = 6, columnspan = 2 )

# Static Properties:
window.title( 'Lotto Number Picker' )
window.resizable( 0, 0 )
getBtn.configure( text = 'Get My Lucky Numbers' )
resBtn.configure( text = 'Reset' )

# Initial Properties:
label1.configure( text = '...' )
label2.configure( text = '...' )
label3.configure( text = '...' )
label4.configure( text = '...' )
label5.configure( text = '...' )
label6.configure( text = '...' )
resBtn.configure( state = DISABLED )

# Dynamic Properties:
from random import sample

def pick() :
        nums = sample( range( 1, 59 ), 6 )
        label1.configure( text = nums[0] )
        label2.configure( text = nums[1] )
        label3.configure( text = nums[2] )
        label4.configure( text = nums[3] )
        label5.configure( text = nums[4] )
        label6.configure( text = nums[5] )
        getBtn.configure( state = DISABLED )
        resBtn.configure( state = NORMAL )

def reset() :
        label1.configure( text = '...' )
        label2.configure( text = '...' )
        label3.configure( text = '...' )
        label4.configure( text = '...' )
        label5.configure( text = '...' )
        label6.configure( text = '...' )
        getBtn.configure( state = NORMAL )
        resBtn.configure( state = DISABLED )

getBtn.configure( command = pick )
resBtn.configure( command = reset )

# Sustain window:
window.mainloop()
                                                          Ln: 1  Col: 0
```

It is convention to place all **import** statements at the start of the script but they can appear anywhere, as listed here.

The color highlighting in the IDLE editor differs from that used throughout this book – but the code precisely compares to that listed in this chapter's steps.

Testing the program

Having worked through the program plan on the previous pages, the widgets needed and functionality required have now been added to the application – so it's ready to be tested.

1 Launch the application and examine its initial appearance

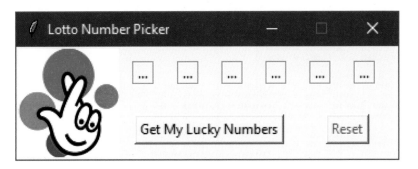

Static text appears on the window title bar and on the Button widgets, the window's resize button is disabled, the small Labels contain their initial ellipsis text values, and the "Reset" button is in its initial disabled state.

2 Next, click the "Get My Lucky Numbers" Button widget – to execute all the statements within the **pick()** function

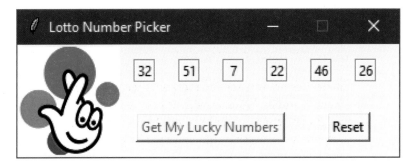

No number is repeated in any series because the random module's **sample()** function returns a set of <u>unique</u> random integers.

A series of numbers within the desired range is displayed and the Button states have changed as required – a further series of numbers cannot be generated until the application has been reset.

3 Make a note of the numbers generated in this first series for comparison later

4 Click the "Reset" Button widget – to execute all the statements within the **reset()** function and see the application resume its initial appearance as required

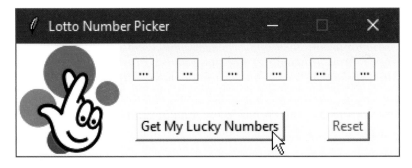

5 Click the "Get My Lucky Numbers" Button widget again – to execute its **pick()** function again and confirm that the new series of numbers differ from the first series

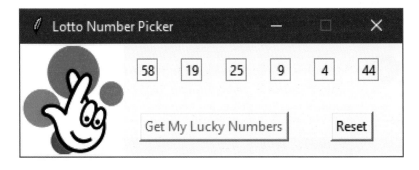

6 Finally, restart the application and click the "Get My Lucky Numbers" Button widget once more – and confirm that this first series numbers are different to those noted in the first series when the application last ran

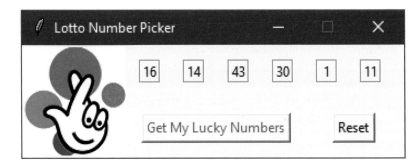

The series of generated numbers are not repeated each time the application gets launched because the random generator is seeded by the current system time – which is different each time the generator gets called upon.

Hot tip

You can discover more about PyInstaller and get help online at **pyinstaller.org**

Don't forget

The pip program will only be available at the command prompt if the Python directory such as C:\Python37 was added to your system's PATH – see page 11 for details. You can discover more about the pip program online at **pip.pypa.io**

Installing a freezing tool

Having satisfactorily tested the application on paged 180-181, you may wish to distribute it for use on other computers where the Python interpreter has not necessarily been installed. To ensure the application will execute successfully without the Python interpreter, your program files can be "frozen" into a bundle within a single stand-alone executable file.

The "PyInstaller" tool is a free program for freezing Python scripts into executables for Windows, Linux, or Mac. There are 32-bit and 64-bit versions of PyInstaller available for Windows, Linux, and macOS/Mac OS X, but these are not cross-platform tools. This means they will only produce an executable file for that same operating system. For example, PyInstaller for Windows will only produce an executable (.exe) file for the Windows operating system.

The PyInstaller tool is a package that can be installed from the Python Package Index ("PyPI") – the default package index of the Python community, which is available to all Python developers. Installation of packages from PyPI is easily implemented using the "pip" command line program that should be automatically included in the Scripts folder of your Python directory:

1 To confirm pip is available, launch a Command Prompt window and enter the command **pip -h** – the program should respond with its list of commands

```
Command Prompt                                          —    □    ✕

C:\MyScripts>pip -h

Usage:
  pip <command> [options]

Commands:
  install                      Install packages.
  download                     Download packages.
  uninstall                    Uninstall packages.
  freeze                       Output installed packages in requirements format.
  list                         List installed packages.
  ...
```

2 Ensure you have an internet connection, then enter the command **pip install pyinstaller** to install the freezing tool

```
Command Prompt                                          —    □    ✕

C:\MyScripts>pip install pyinstaller
Collecting pyinstaller
Installing collected packages: pyinstaller
  Running setup.py install for pyinstaller ... done
Successfully installed pyinstaller

C:\MyScripts>_
```

3 After PyInstaller has successfully installed, enter the command **pyinstaller -h** to list the PyInstaller arguments – see a script name is always required as the final argument

```
Command Prompt                                          —    □    ×

C:\MyScripts>pyinstaller -h
usage: pyinstaller [-h] [-v] ...  scriptname

positional arguments:
  scriptname               name of scriptfiles to be processed
```

4 Scroll down the list to find the "What to generate" section – see a **--onefile** option to generate a single file

```
Command Prompt                                          —    □    ×

What to generate:
  -D, --onedir           Create a one-folder bundle containing an executable
                         (default)
  -F, --onefile          Create a one-file bundled executable.
  --specpath DIR         Folder to store the generated spec file (default:
                         current directory)
  -n NAME, --name NAME   Name to assign to the bundled app and spec file
                         (default: first script's basename)
```

You will need to use the four highlighted options depicted here to create an executable version of the Lotto program.

5 Scroll further down the list to the "What to bundle" section – see a **--add-binary** option to include image files

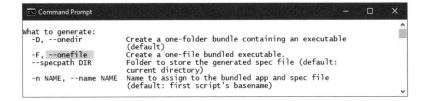

```
Command Prompt                                          —    □    ×

What to bundle, where to search:
  --add-data <SRC;DEST or SRC:DEST>
                         Additional non-binary files or folders to be added to
                         the executable. The path separator is platform
                         specific, ``os.pathsep`` (which is ``;`` on Windows
                         and ``:`` on most unix systems) is used. This option
                         can be used multiple times.
  --add-binary <SRC;DEST or SRC:DEST>
                         Additional binary files to be added to the executable.
```

6 Scroll further down the list to the "Windows options" section – see a **--noconsole** option to suppress the console

```
Command Prompt                                          —    □    ×

Windows and Mac OS X specific options:
  -c, --console, --nowindowed
                         Open a console window for standard i/o (default)
  -w, --windowed, --noconsole
                         Windows and Mac OS X: do not provide a console window
                         for standard i/o. On Mac OS X this also triggers
                         building an OS X .app bundle.
  -i, --icon <FILE.ico or FILE.exe.ID or FILE.icns>
                         FILE.ico: apply that icon to a Windows executable.
```

Also notice the **--icon** option, which can be used to specify the path to an icon (.ico) file include for the generated executable program.

Freezing the program

Applications developed in the Python language can be frozen for Windows, Linux, and Mac systems using the PyInstaller tool, introduced on pages 182-183, to create a single standalone executable file. Apps that require the inclusion of additional files, such as image files, require the script file to be modified so the PyInstaller tool can readily locate them at their absolute address:

184

1 Open the **lotto.py** program file and add this utility function definition at the very start of the script

```
def resource_path( relative_path ) :
        absolute_path = os.path.abspath( __file__ )
        root_path = os.path.dirname( absolute_path )
        base_path = getattr( sys, 'MEIPASS', root_path )
        return os.path.join( base_path, relative_path )
```

2 Modify the assignment to the **img** variable – to identify the image file's location using the added utility function

```
img = PhotoImage( file = resource_path( 'logo.gif' ) )
```

```
lucky.py - C:\MyScripts\lucky.py                          —    □    ×
File  Edit  Format  Run  Options  Window  Help
def resource_path( relative_path ) :
        absolute_path = os.path.abspath( __file__ )
        root_path = os.path.dirname( absolute_path )
        base_path = getattr( sys, '_MEIPASS', root_path )
        return os.path.join( base_path, relative_path )

# Widgets:
from tkinter import *
window = Tk()
img = PhotoImage( file = resource_path('logo.gif') )
                                                      Ln: 10  Col: 52
```

lucky.py

3 Save the modified file as "lucky.py" in your MyScripts folder, then open a Command Prompt in that folder

4 Begin a command with **pyinstaller --onefile --noconsole** to instruct PyInstaller to create a single file, and to prevent the program also opening a console window

5 Continue the command with **--add-binary logo.gif;.** to include the image file in the single executable

6 Complete the command with the **lucky.py** script name – so the command now looks like that on the opposite page

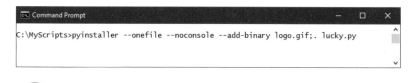

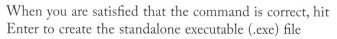

7 When you are satisfied that the command is correct, hit Enter to create the standalone executable (.exe) file

8 PyInstaller creates two folders named "build" and "dist" within your MyScripts folder. The standalone executable file can be found in the "dist" folder

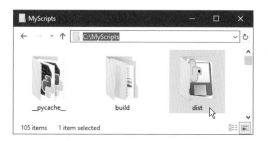

9 The executable file can be distributed to other users who do not have Python installed, and the program can be run from a command line or by double-clicking its file icon

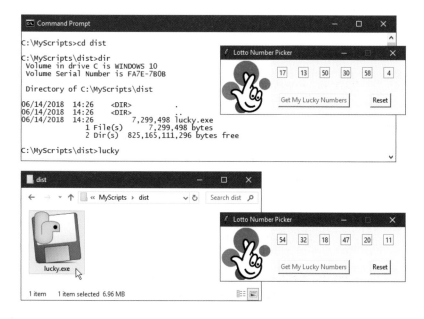

Beware

The items following the **--add-binary** argument specify the file name (**logo.gif**) and desired destination (. for current directory) separated by a ; semicolon character. Unix systems must use a : colon character as this separator.

Hot tip

PyInstaller bundles a copy of all files required by the script (including the Python interpreter) into one executable file. This means its requirements may vary. For help and more details please refer to the PyInstaller Manual at **pyinstaller.readthedocs.io**

Summary

- The standard Python library has a **random** module that provides functions to generate pseudo-random numbers.

- A pseudo-random floating-point number from 0.0 to 1.0 can be generated by the **random** module's **random()** function.

- Multiple unique random integers within a given range can be generated by the **random** module's **sample()** function.

- A program plan should define the program's purpose, required functionality, and interface widgets needed.

- In designing a program interface, the **grid()** layout manager positions widgets in rows and columns.

- Static properties <u>do not</u> change during execution of a program.

- Dynamic properties <u>do</u> change during execution of a program using runtime functionality to respond to a user action.

- Upon completion, a program should be tested to ensure it performs as expected in every respect.

- Program files can be "frozen" into a bundle for distribution to other computers where the Python interpreter is not present.

- The PyInstaller tool can be used to freeze programs into executables for Windows, Mac, or Linux.

- The **pyinstaller** command's **--onefile** argument specifies that it should create a single executable file.

- The **pyinstaller** command's **--noconsole** argument specifies that the executable file should not also produce a console window.

- The **pyinstaller** command's **--add-binary** argument can specify image files to be bundled within the executable file.

- When bundling image files their absolute path address on the system must be specified within the program script.

Index

生 4 Venture Suite 255
92618